U.S. AND SOVIET SPACE PROGRAMS

U.S.
AND
Soviet
SPACE PROGRAMS
A COMPARISON
David E. Newton

FRANKLIN WATTS|1988
NEW YORK|LONDON|TORONTO|SYDNEY

Cover photograph courtesy of

All photographs courtesy of NASA except: UPI/Bettmann Newsphotos:
pp. 12, 64 (bottom right—NASA), 91 (both—NASA); Tass from
Sovfoto: pp. 14, 26, 42 (both), 51 (bottom left and right), 62,
(both), 79, 82, 84, 85, 105 (both); New York Public Library Picture
Collection: p. 74; Los Alamos National Laboratory: p. 125.

Library of Congress Cataloging-in-Publication Data

Newton, David E.
  U.S. and Soviet space programs.

  (An Impact book)
  Bibliography: p.
  Includes index.
  Summary: Surveys the history of the space race
between the United States and the Soviet Union,
discussing similarities and differences in the
goals, methods, and innovations of the two nations'
space programs.
    1. Astronautics—United States—History—Juvenile
literature. 2. Astronautics—Soviet Union—History—
Juvenile literature. [1. Astronautics—United States—
History. 2. Astronautics—Soviet Union—History]
I. Title.
TL789.8.U5N44   1988   387.8'0973   87-23024
ISBN 0-531-10515-6

CONTENTS

This book is
gratefully dedicated to
Dr. Pat Gozemba,
for making her own life
an inspiration and a
challenge, and
for being a good friend.

OTHER BOOKS BY
DAVID E. NEWTON

Science Ethics
Science and Social Issues
Nutrition for You
Understanding Venereal Disease
Chemistry Updated
Biology Updated
Sexual Health
An Introduction to Molecular Biology
Learning Facts and Attitudes about Human Sexuality
Sexual Questions
Knowledge for a Nuclear World

U.S. AND SOVIET SPACE PROGRAMS

1
THE BEGINNINGS

Beep, beep; beep, beep. The timid, cricketlike radio signal came from a small satellite orbiting high above the earth's surface. Hardly the trumpet fanfare one might expect to mark the opening of a new age in human civilization! Yet, *Sputnik*—Russian for "traveler"—was just that. This tiny space traveler was the first artificial earth satellite to be placed in earth orbit.

Launched from the Soviet spaceflight center at Tyuratam on October 4, 1957, *Sputnik* traveled in an elliptical orbit ranging from 227 to 947 km (142 to 592 mi) in height. The 83.6-kg (186-lb) metal sphere completed one pass around the earth every ninety-six minutes. During each of its trips around the globe, it passed over a new part of the earth, sending its simple message of greeting to observers in the United States and Europe, to its own citizens, and to nearly every part of the world. Within hours, the whole world knew of the Soviets' historic accomplishment.

Most earthbound listeners could hardly have been more surprised. The Soviets had long been respected for their courage and strong national pride. But few non-Russians thought of the Soviet Union as a modern, advanced, technologically powerful nation. How could this backward, ag-

Sputnik, *mounted on a stand, before being launched*

ricultural society, so recently devastated by the war, have the scientific know-how to achieve this remarkable breakthrough?

Skeptics looked for ways to reconcile the reality of *Sputnik* with their image of a primitive Soviet technology. Perhaps the launch succeeded, they guessed, only after many failures. Or maybe the Soviet achievement was really the work of German rocket scientists captured at the end of World War II. Or had the clever Soviets found a way to carry out a massive hoax, and *Sputnik* never really existed at all?

These doubting Thomases had seriously underestimated the Soviet space program. Bits of evidence existed to show that the Soviets had long been serious about their space program. In the first place, the Soviets had been warning about a possible satellite launch for months.

They, like the United States, had hoped to orbit the first artificial satellite in connection with the International Geophysical Year (IGY), which ran from July 1, 1957, to December 31, 1958 (an eighteen-month "year"). In fact, the Soviet magazine *Radio* had even announced the frequencies on which the satellite could be heard. And the magazine described to radio operators throughout the world the orbital characteristics of the forthcoming satellite and the best ways to detect its signals.

Besides, the Soviet Union already had a long history of interest in space travel. The founding father of Soviet space research, Konstantin Tsiolkovsky, had written about and experimented with space vehicles for at least four decades before his death in 1935. As early as 1903, for example, he had worked out the mathematics for keeping a satellite in orbit, and he designed a rocket that would operate on liquid oxygen and hydrogen.

And everyone involved in space research knew of the fierce race at the end of World War II to capture the German scientists working on the V-2 rocket. Although the United States had won that race for most of the upper-level scientists, the Soviets still found hundreds of qualified technicians, some rocket plans, and a few rockets themselves, all hauled back to the Soviet Union.

Finally, the Soviets had already completed research on very large rockets, machines big enough to carry bombs from the Soviet Union to the United States. These intercontinental ballistic missiles (ICBMs) were the Soviets' answer to U.S. mastery of nuclear weapons.

U.S. military experts tended to downplay the importance of the Soviet ICBMs, calling them "massive and clumsy." They thought that Soviet engineers lacked the skills to produce devices (like a satellite) that were "delicate, requiring deft precision and true craftsmanship."[1] In fact, the powerful ICBMs had the capability of carrying more than bombs to an enemy nation; they were able to launch satellites into orbit around the earth. So the first successful ICBM tests in August 1957 meant that space flights might not be far behind.

For anyone who still doubted the Soviet Union's com-

Konstantin Tsiolkovsky, the father of Soviet space research

mitment to space travel—and its ability to follow up on that commitment—the months following the launch of *Sputnik 1* were even more of an eye-opener. Only a month later, on November 3, 1957, the Soviets launched a second satellite.

Sputnik 2 weighed six times as much—508.3 kg (1,120 lb)—as its older sister and carried the first animal—a dog named Laika—into space. Biomedical data collected on Laika during launch and seven days in orbit provided some of the first information needed to begin planning for manned spaceflights. No plans for recovering *Sputnik 2* were made. Laika either suffocated from lack of oxygen or was poisoned after the week of experiments. The satellite itself continued in orbit for another 155 days.

Then, on May 15, 1958, the Soviets launched yet a third satellite. *Sputnik 3* was even more massive, 1,327 kg (2,926 lb). It was the first orbiting geophysical laboratory designed to collect and transmit data on charged particles in the earth's atmosphere, solar radiation, interplanetary dust, and the earth's magnetic field.

No one could deny the enormous scientific and technological achievement represented by *Sputnik 1, 2,* and *3*. Clearly, any notions that the Soviet Union was "backward" or "technologically undeveloped" were outmoded and out of touch with reality.

THE POLITICAL IMPACT OF *SPUTNIK*

The *Sputnik*s were more than a *technological* success. The Soviets were very clear that this technological accomplishment had social and political meaning. The success of the *Sputnik*s was tied to and came about, they insisted, because of the superiority of the socialist system. At every possible point, Soviet politicians, space scientists, and journalists pointed out the connection between the Soviet space successes and the Soviet form of government. As one official statement of the Communist party of the Soviet Union proclaimed: "These victories [in space research] epitomize the advantages of the Socialist system, its successes in economic competition with capitalism, the creative genius of the Soviet people, the correctness of the policy of the CPSU, the triumph of the ideas of Marxism-Leninism."[2]

Soviet political scholars pointed out that communism provided the best possible setting for the growth and development of science and technology. As Mstislav Keldysh, president of the USSR Academy of Sciences, put it:

> The most advanced social system, [that which] merged science to communism into one whole, creates the most favorable conditions for material and intellectual progress. . . . [A]rmed with revolutionary Marxist-Leninist theory . . . [the Soviet Union] has taken a leading position in some very important scientific fields. A clear example of the development level of Soviet science and engineering are the successes achieved in space exploration. . . .[3]

Thus, the Soviets claimed that success in space provided confirmation that communism was, indeed, the best form of government. From the earliest days of its space programs, technological achievements and national prestige became intertwined. A successful new spacecraft meant new glory for the Motherland. Failures (if and when they were acknowledged) were social and political—as well as engineering—disasters.

The *Sputnik* success was to have long-term propaganda value. As one scholar has put it: "In a matter of days and weeks after *Sputnik* every propaganda theme of the next seven years was coined and in circulation."[4]

For example, by the early 1960s the Soviets were using their space program as a crucial bargaining chip and selling point in their interaction with developing and uncommitted nations. In the contest with the United States for the hearts and minds of Third World peoples, the Soviets made the most of their space successes. They argued that communism and science, working hand in hand, provided a means by which people could overcome their backwardness, "reach for the stars," and spur their own development.

Speaking on this theme, Premier Nikita Khruschev reminded the world how this partnership had worked for the Soviet Union and, presumably, could work for other developing nations as well:

[Capitalist statesmen] used to make fun of us, saying that we Russians were running about in bark sandals and lapping up cabbage soup with those sandals. . . . Then, suddenly, you understand those who they thought lapped up cabbage soup with bark sandals go into outer space earlier than the so-called civilized ones."[5]

Thus, at all points in its history, the Soviet space program has been more than a scientific and engineering project. It has also been a way of confirming the correctness of socialism and communism, a source of national pride, and a contributor to national prestige.

REACTION IN THE UNITED STATES
American reaction to *Sputnik* was mixed. Scientists had known for some time that they were in a "space race" with the Soviets. Both nations had announced in July 1955 their intentions to launch a satellite during the forthcoming International Geophysical Year. So scientists in the United States were disappointed, but not completely surprised, that they had lost that race.

NATION IS WARNED TO STRESS SCIENCE

Faces Doom Unless Youth
Learns Its Importance,
Chief Physicist Says

HARRIMAN SCORES U.S. SATELLITE LAG

Says Administration Holds
Up Funds by Complacency
—Stevenson in Warning

U.S. DELAY DRAWS SCIENTISTS' FIRE

Satellite Lag Laid to the
Withholding of Money
and Waste of Time

Sputnik-*inspired headlines*

Members of the Eisenhower administration were taken somewhat aback when they learned of the Soviet accomplishment. But most did not regard the achievement as particularly significant. President Eisenhower himself referred to *Sputnik 1* as "one small ball in the air, something that does not raise my apprehensions, not one iota."

But the president had gravely misjudged the impact of *Sputnik* on American journalists, the average citizen, and the U.S. Congress. From every corner voices were raised about the sudden Soviet "threat in space." Critics interpreted the success of *Sputnik* as an indication that American science was falling apart, that the military was not prepared to defend the nation, and that our educational system had failed the nation. The government's response to these fears and complaints was to dramatically reshape the nature of these three institutions over the next decade.

2

THE
UNITED STATES
RESPONDS

By the end of 1957, Americans were not feeling very good about their space program (or their military stance or their scientific research or their educational system!). One cause for this concern was the great success of the Soviet *Sputnik* launches. But another reason for the nation's dissatisfaction was the dramatic failures of early U.S. rocket launches carried out at about the same time as the *Sputnik* successes.

Like the Soviets, the United States had made no secret about its plans to launch an artificial earth satellite during the IGY. And, until October 1957, American scientists still thought they had a good chance of being first in space with a satellite. After the appearance of *Sputnik 1,* however, they knew they had to settle for second best.

Even so, those scientists counted on salvaging American prestige with a launch of their own satellite, code-named *Vanguard TV-3,* in December 1957. The U.S. satellite was a bit anemic—a tiny 1.4-kg (3.1-lb) metal ball, which compared poorly in size with the giant 83.6-kg (184-lb) *Sputnik 2* already in orbit. But the smaller *Vanguard* was, in many ways, technologically more advanced than either the primitive *Sputnik 1* or the bulky, but simple, *Sputnik 2.*

Hopes were high on December 6, when engineers ignited the rocket that would launch both the *Vanguard* satellite and the U.S. space program. Those hopes were quickly dashed. The rocket rose about a meter off the launchpad, was engulfed in flames, and fell crashing back to earth. The U.S. failure, unlike Soviet launches then and now, was witnessed by reporters from across the nation and around the world. National embarrassment was the order of the day! (To rub salt into the wound, a Soviet delegate at the United Nations asked his U.S. counterpart if the Soviets could help the U.S. space program under its Aid to Underdeveloped Nations program!)

EARLY HISTORY OF
THE U.S. SPACE PROGRAM

Until the disastrous collapse of *Vanguard,* U.S. and Soviet space programs had had a remarkably similar history. The U.S. counterpart of Soviet space pioneer Tsiolkovsky was Robert Goddard. Goddard had developed an interest in rocketry early in life, while still a physics student at Clark University in 1899. In what may have been the U.S. government's first contribution to space research, the Smithsonian Institution gave Goddard five thousand dollars in 1916 to build experimental rockets.

Goddard's first success did not come until ten years later, however. On March 16, 1926, he launched a rocket fueled by oxygen and gasoline to an altitude of 12.5 m (41.0 ft) in 2.5 seconds, at an average velocity of 96.6 km/hr (60.4 mi/hr). Until his death in 1945, Goddard continued to make improvements in rocket design, eventually producing a model scarcely different from the German V-2 model used during World War II.

As that war neared its end in early 1945, U.S. military scientists, like their Soviet counterparts, were eager to get their hands on the German V-2 researchers. They designed a plan, called Operation Paperclip, to recruit the V-2 specialists before they could be reached by the Soviets.

The Americans had a great advantage in this race, for most of the German rocket scientists had decided that

they *preferred* to fall prisoner to the U.S. Army. They reasoned that their chances for continuing their studies of rockets and spaceflight would be greater in the United States than in the USSR.

So on May 2, 1945, an English-speaking German, Magnus von Braun, surrendered himself, more than five hundred V-2 scientists, over a ton of V-2 research documents, and countless parts of V-2 rockets to a surprised United States private. Probably the most important prize in that surrender was Magnus von Braun's brother, Wernher, who was to become perhaps the most important single person in the U.S. space program over the next four decades.

THE FIRST U.S. SATELLITE

Now heir to the highly successful V-2 project, the United States had a great early advantage in its efforts to open the space age. By the 1950s, the U.S. space program was operating with one major handicap, however. Its organization was fragmented among three branches of the military services: the army, the air force, and the navy.

Von Braun and his fellow German scientists were working for the "Orbiter" program of the Army Ballistic Missile Agency (ABMA) in Huntsville, Alabama. They proposed using a modified Redstone rocket to launch their version of an artificial earth satellite during the IGY. The navy team's Vanguard program offered a less powerful booster— an upgraded Viking rocket—but a more sophisticated satellite. Finally, the air force was working on perhaps the most powerful rocket booster of all—an Atlas ICBM— although its program was less developed than either the army's or navy's.

The final choice as to which service was to have the honor of launching the first U.S. satellite was decided in a characteristically American way: by committee. The Stewart Committee, consisting of eight prominent scien-

Robert Goddard, the father of
American rocketry, in 1925

tists, faced a difficult choice among three competing programs, each of which had something to recommend it. Eventually, three committee members voted for the Vanguard and two for the Redstone. Two other members felt that they didn't know enough about rockets to vote, so agreed with the majority. One member was ill and did not vote.

The decision to bypass von Braun's Orbiter project was a great shock to the army team, as well as to many other U.S. rocket experts. And the failure of *Vanguard* in December 1957 was only the first bit of proof that the navy had been asked to accomplish more than it was ready to do. A backup Viking (TV-3BU) was prepared for a second launch attempt. But additional problems delayed that launch until February 1958. When the lift-off finally did occur on February 5, the rocket went off course and had to be destroyed only fifty-seven seconds after launch. Overall, the navy Vanguard program was a distinct disappointment, with only three successful launches out of eleven attempts in its lifetime.

U.S. space officials soon decided that their choice of the navy had been a mistake. Only five days after *Sputnik 2* appeared in orbit, Dr. von Braun and his army team were told to renew work on their Orbiter program. It took little time for the von Braun team to respond to this order because they had never really stopped their research after the Stewart Committee's decision two years earlier. In less than three months the army team had given the United States its first satellite, *Explorer 1.*

Compared to the *Sputnik*s still in space, *Explorer 1* was something of a "lightweight." It measured 4.8 kg (11 lb), only 5 percent of the weight of *Sputnik 1* and less than 1 percent of the weight of *Sputnik 2.* Of greater significance, however, was the satellite's scientific capabilities. Both *Sputnik*s were little more than hollow balls. *Sputnik 1* carried a recording device, although the Soviets apparently did little with the data received, and *Sputnik 2* carried both life-support and transmission equipment.

On the other hand, *Explorer 1* carried equipment that allowed it to measure cosmic ray intensities, atmospheric

One of the Vanguard *satellites (U.S.)*

temperatures, micrometeoroid collisions, and radiation levels. Within days of reaching orbit on January 31, 1958, the U.S. satellite had sent back news of the first real scientific discovery in space, the existence of radiation belts (named the "Van Allen" belts) surrounding the earth.

The army launched four more *Explorers* during 1958. Two of these failed to reach orbit, while two provided further information on the earth's upper atmosphere. To add a bright chapter to an otherwise dismal story, the navy's first successful Vanguard flight reached orbit on March 17, 1958. It sent back data which allowed scientists to determine that the earth is pear-shaped, rather than spherical.

After a difficult and discouraging start, the U.S. space program had finally begun to produce results.

3

THE TWO SPACE PROGRAMS

The launches of *Sputniks*, *Explorers*, and *Vanguards* all had one thing in common: They resulted from major, expensive, government-financed programs. The days when a Tsiolkovsky or a Goddard could send up homemade rockets at the cost of a few thousand dollars or rubles had, by 1957, long passed.

For more than three decades in both the Soviet Union and the United States, space research has been a vital and very expensive function of each nation's government. The fruits of this research are essential to each nation's military program to its scientific progress, and to its prestige in world affairs.

The organization and administration of space research in the two nations is, however, quite different. In each country, the way in which decisions are made and carried out reflects that government's political philosophy. In the United States, debates over space policy are carried out, for the most part, in public view where legislators, scientists, and average citizens can follow what decisions are made and how they are being made. In the Soviet Union, such decisions tend to be formulated by a relatively small number of individuals accountable only to the formal party and governmental apparatus itself, not to the general public.

SPACE POLICY IN
THE SOVIET UNION

In fact, any discussion of decision-making on space issues in the Soviet Union is restricted by how little we really know about the way the Soviet space program is organized, financed, and administered. As with many aspects of their society, the Soviets withhold a good deal of information about their space program.

For example, the Soviet custom has usually been not to announce a flight until *after* (sometimes, *long after*) it has reached orbit successfully. If the launch fails, the Soviets may simply pretend that the launch never took place. (More recently, with the availability of better tracking equipment, the Soviets are pressed to account for all their launches.)

This secrecy extends even to the existence and location of two of the three major Soviet launch sites. The busiest launchpad in the Soviet Union—indeed, in the world—is located near the village of Plesetsk. This site was not even acknowledged by the Soviets until 1983, seventeen years after it was first used for satellite launching.

Even then, the government mentioned its existence only because nearby residents had become extraordinarily alarmed by what they thought were UFOs. Since 1983, Plesetsk has slipped back into oblivion, escaping further mention in the official Soviet press.

The Soviets do acknowledge the second launch site . . . but they give it the name of a village more than 300 km (200 mi) away from its actual location. The "Baikonur cosmodrome" is, in fact, just outside the village of Tyuratam. Even official Soviet documents provided to the International Astronautical Federation in Paris list the location of this site as 48.2° north latitude and 75.5° east longitude, instead of its correct 45.9° north latitude and 63.3° east longitude.

Given the secrecy of the Soviet program, how do outside observers get their information about the purpose of launches, successes, and failures? Sometimes the answer to that question reads like a good (if very complex) detective story. Western observers collect information from

U.S. "spy" satellites, from our own worldwide telemetry systems, and from amateur and professional ground-based observers. Then they work backward using the information collected to calculate the location of a launch, the time of lift-off, orbital characteristics, and, based on these data, the probable purpose of the launch.

For example, most satellites with the same purpose are likely to have very similar launch and orbital characteristics. We might know, for instance, that the Soviets tend to launch earth resource satellites from the Kapustin Yar cosmodrome by means of an A-2 rocket into an orbit ranging from about 215 to 275 km (134 to 170 mi), with an orbital period of about eighty-nine minutes. If observers detect an unannounced Soviet launch with all of these characteristics, they may infer that the mysterious satellite was part of the Soviet earth resources program.

Perhaps the most interesting group of Soviet space detectives are those working at and with the Kettering Boys School in Northants, England. For more than two decades, Geoffrey E. Perry, physics head at the school, has directed the school's amateur space sleuths. The Kettering group eavesdrops on Soviet satellite signals, observes their flight paths, watches for patterns in these data, and predicts the nature and function of many otherwise unidentified Soviet flights. Perry's students, former students, and friends throughout the world all contribute to the remarkable success of this project.

Information about the Soviet space program also comes from speeches by Soviet officials, newspaper and magazine articles, government documents, and reports from people who have emigrated from the Soviet Union. The problem is that these sources often provide conflicting information.

For example, Western observers held quite different views in 1970 as to whether the Soviet Union had ever

The Baikonur cosmo-drome near Tyuratam, in the Soviet Union

intended to land humans on the moon. Those on both sides of that argument could point to official Soviet reports and speeches that supported their case.

Even when the Soviets do speak clearly on a space issue, their words may need to be examined carefully. For example, Soviet leaders have always insisted that the objectives of their space program are entirely peaceful and scientific. Yet outside observers are thoroughly convinced that military objectives are an important part of—possibly the driving force behind—the Soviet space program.

THE ORGANIZATION OF THE SOVIET SPACE PROGRAM

Much of what is written about the philosophy, policies, organization, financing, and administration of the Soviet space program should therefore be qualified with a "perhaps" or a "probably." One point about which we can be relatively certain is that overall Soviet space policy is formulated at the very top, by whoever is the Soviet leader at any particular time. That policy is probably discussed and affirmed by the nation's highest policy-making body, the Politburo of the Communist party of the Soviet Union (CPSU). Apparently, one member of the Politburo has a special interest in and responsibility for space matters.

Western observers have long argued as to whether the Soviet Union has a NASA-like central coordinating body for its space programs. Even today, we don't know the answer to that question. An official U.S. government report on this issue claims that "there is evidence and strong opinion on both sides, but no proof."[6]

The agency within the Soviet government (in contrast to the Communist party) responsible for space matters is the State Committee on Science and Technology (SCST). Outside observers disagree as to what role and responsibilities the SCST has. The consensus seems to be that the Committee is the most likely candidate as the chief coordinating body for the space program.

In all likelihood, the Soviets draw on many agencies in the operation of their space program. For example, Soviet officials have claimed that the Soviet Academy of Sciences is their equivalent of NASA. In negotiations with the United States and other nations, the Soviet Union is generally represented by members of the Academy. Military agencies are also active in the Soviet space program. All rocket launches—for both military and civilian purposes—are conducted by the Strategic Rocket Force of the Ministry of Defense, and cosmonaut training is conducted by the Soviet Air Force.

THE U.S. SPACE PROGRAM

We know a good deal more about the U.S. space program than we do about its Soviet counterpart. From its inception, NASA has conscientiously recorded the ongoing debates as to what the purpose of our space program ought to be and how that program should be organized, administered, and financed.

One thing was clear at the very outset, however: The U.S. space program would be different in some fundamental ways from the Soviet program. To be sure, the Soviet model had much to recommend itself. A system in which no dissent is allowed can be highly efficient. Government decisions and directives can be put into effect without having to worry about disputes or disagreements from scientists, legislators, or the general public. When some technological objective is the goal—for example, sending a man to the moon—that system can be highly efficient and, therefore, very appealing to the rulers of a nation.

But most U.S. officials have always recognized that the Soviet model is not appropriate for this nation. Our political philosophy requires that policy decisions be openly debated, arrived at by consensus, and subject to change. Secretary of State John Foster Dulles observed in the first year of the new Space Age that the Soviets "have a good big start on us" because their projects are "the products of despotisms . . . not the product of a democratic way of life."[7]

In fact, one feature of the U.S. space program is that it has always been at the mercy of shifting national moods.

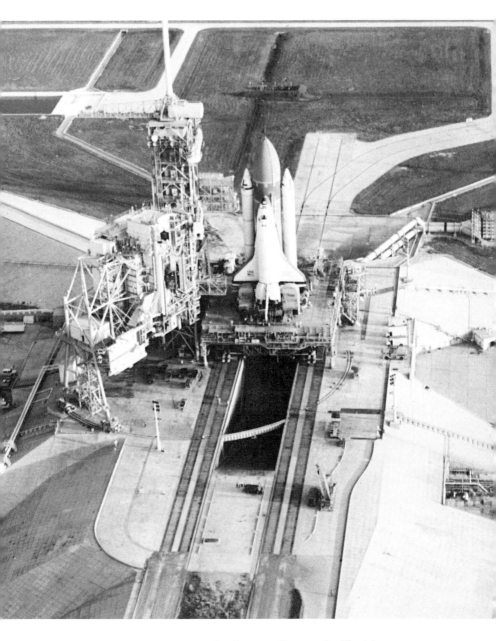

The Kennedy Space Center in Florida

A recent analysis by the Office of Technology Assessment (OTA) has pointed out that

> the space program has . . . been directed by political and budgetary pressures not always relevant to a logically ordered exploration and use of space. At the same time, none of the policymaking bodies successively established in the executive branch nor any of the congressional committees have been able to ensure that a long-range plan of particular policies and programs would be pursued.[8]

In commenting about this report, the director of the OTA explained that "the problem is that NASA has sort of translated [its job] into a series of manned, human-related projects, loosely strung together, and has either not been allowed to or has not developed a rational, well articulated explanation of goals in space."[9]

Nonetheless, American politicians in the later 1950s were confronted with a specific, concrete pair of questions about space research. The first question was what the U.S. philosophy about space was to be. Between 1952 and 1960, that question was answered by the Republican administration of President Dwight D. Eisenhower.

President Eisenhower's philosophy about space has been described as "calm conservatism."[10] Unlike Soviet leaders, Eisenhower did not believe that space research served any political ends. He did not see *Sputnik* or *Explorer* as bargaining chips between the two superpowers or in negotiations with other nations. Also unlike the Soviets, he insisted that military and civilian space projects be kept distinctly separate from each other. He assigned military programs to the Department of Defense and proposed the creation of a new agency to handle civilian space research.

Eisenhower received strong support for his position from American scientists. In a 1958 report entitled *Introduction to Outer Space*, the President's Science Advisory Committee (PSAC) proposed a national space program that would emphasize scientific research. The report showed little interest in diplomatic ramifications of the space program and emphasized the importance of other national scientific priorities over space objectives.

PSAC's philosophy was summarized in its recommendation that "it would not be in the national interest to exploit space science at the cost of weakening our efforts in other scientific endeavors. This need not happen if we plan our national program for space science and technology as part of a balanced national effort in all science and technology."[11]

This issue has continued to trouble many scientists ever since the dawn of the Space Age. In debates over space research, their concern has always been that a mammoth space program with a significant political objective would tend to draw financial resources away from more worthy, but less dramatic, scientific research.

Eisenhower's concept of an American space program faced stiff opposition, however, from three quarters: the aerospace industry, the army and air force, and some politicians. Each group had its own special interests in a space program different from the president's concept. The aerospace industry, for example, was, quite naturally, eager to see a far more ambitious program than the president had in mind. The military services chafed at the second-class status to which his emphasis on a civilian program would have assigned them. And politicians (led by Senate Majority Leader Lyndon B. Johnson) were distressed at Eisenhower's apparent lack of concern about the nation's loss of prestige because of the *Sputnik* launch.

FORMATION OF NASA

The battleground for the conflict between Eisenhower and his supporters on the one hand and the military, Senator Johnson, and their allies on the other was the president's recommendation, sent to Congress on April 4, 1958, for a new national space agency. For more than three months, the House and Senate argued over the president's plan and the alternate proposals developed by each house. Finally, on July 16, 1958, a compromise bill was passed and, thirteen days later, signed by the president.

The legislation created a new civilian space agency, the National Aeronautics and Space Administration (NASA), which was to be guided by six policy principles:

1. That U.S. preeminence in space science and applications be maintained
2. That economic and social benefits be derived
3. That knowledge be increased
4. That civilian and military activities be separated (though they are to be coordinated and are not to duplicate one another unnecessarily)
5. That the National Aeronautics and Space Administration (NASA), the civilian agency, be limited largely to research and development (R&D)
6. That international cooperation be fostered[12]

After stating these principles, the act concentrated on the organization structure that NASA was to have.

Sometimes legislation spells out only what *can* be done, not what *must* be done. Such was the case with the NASA act. During his remaining term of office, President Eisenhower largely ignored the nearly unlimited potential for space research granted by the act. He tended to rely on his own PSAC, rather than NASA's National Aeronautics and Space Council, for advice on space matters.

Overall, he continued to pursue his policy of "calm conservatism" with respect to space. As one observer has written:

Space activity under President Eisenhower was akin to a series of separate and unrelated efforts. NASA conducted interesting experiments in weather and communication satellites and in space science, along with a limited manned project called Mercury. Meanwhile, the Air Force was conducting programs in reconnaissance satellites, communications, and rocket research. Though each had specialized programs producing specific capabilities in a narrow range, there was no overall capability being developed to operate in space for either civilian or military purposes.[13]

KENNEDY RESHAPES THE
U.S. SPACE PROGRAM

The election of John F. Kennedy resulted in a dramatic change in U.S. space policy. Immediately after his election, Kennedy was somewhat unclear as to the direction he had in mind for the U.S. space program. But a series of events in early 1961 helped crystallize his thinking. Probably the most significant of these was the first manned Soviet spaceflight by Yuri Gagarin on April 12 of that year.

Unlike President Eisenhower, Kennedy had come to the conclusion that space research should be a crucial element in the United States' national policy. American foreign policy could be only as effective as our national prestige, Kennedy believed, and that prestige was inextricably linked to our ability to succeed brilliantly in the space race.

In a memo dated May 8, 1961, Vice President Johnson recommended to Kennedy three priorities for the new administration's space program:

1. Accelerated development of rocket boosters
2. More rapid development of communication and meteorological satellites
3. Three projects (the continuation of Mercury, and new Gemini and Apollo programs) which would lead to the landing of an American on the moon

The greatest controversy that developed under Kennedy surrounded the question of manned versus unmanned spaceflight. To the Kennedy administration, the presence of humans in space was absolutely essential for the kind of public-relations space program they wanted. The Soviets had already placed a man in space, and the United States could retain a position of leadership only by doing what the Soviets had done . . . only better. In addition, administration officials hoped that a manned space race with the Soviets would bankrupt that nation's economy, certainly an attractive argument from the U.S. standpoint.

Scientists disagreed with this logic. They argued again (as they had three years earlier) that adding a human to a spacecraft multiplied its costs by as much as a hundred times. Scientifically, it was foolish to divert money from more important scientific projects (including unmanned space projects) in order to carry out what they regarded as a public-relations stunt.

Kennedy found PSAC's arguments unconvincing (in fact, he tended to ignore the committee), and on May 25, 1961, he announced the nation's intention to place a man on the moon before the end of the decade. With that announcement, the focus of the U.S. space program was set for nearly a decade.

HOW NASA OPERATES

Over a period of three decades, NASA has evolved a system for developing and implementing space policy for the United States. That system involves a number of agencies and organizations outside NASA itself. For example, the primary source from which space policy develops is the National Academy of Sciences Space Science Board (SSB). The SSB meets on an irregular basis to consider general goals for space science and to recommend ways of achieving those goals.

Input on space policy may also come from the executive branch of the government, from eighteen other governmental agencies involved in space research, from House and Senate committees and subcommittees, from scientific organizations, industrial groups, and from individual scientists.

Once priorities have been determined, NASA establishes working groups to carry out the projects. Some projects become the responsibility of scientists and engineers who work directly for NASA in installations around the country. Other projects are "farmed out" to universities or private companies. Generally speaking, the greater portion of NASA's work is subcontracted to other agencies. At the peak of the Apollo program, for example, ten to twelve non-NASA people were working on NASA projects for every one NASA employee. By 1981, that rate had dropped to about four non-NASA workers to every one NASA employee.

THE STATUS OF
SPACE RESEARCH TODAY

The difference between the way space science is organized in the Soviet Union and in the United States is dramatically illustrated by the current state of affairs in both countries. By all appearances, the leadership of the Soviet Union has been able to set certain long-term objectives for its space research (such as an orbital space station) and to work toward those objectives efficiently and with considerable success.

The United States has sometimes had comparable successes, the Apollo moon program being perhaps the best example. But the U.S. space program has also been characterized at times by a lack of direction and/or a failure to carry through on objectives. A complaint registered in 1982 by the Office of Technology Assessment is not unusual. The Office reported that "there is no overall agreement about the direction or scope the civilian space program should assume in the future."[14]

Some political scientists argue that this conflict is still one of the most serious policy issues facing the United States today. Can we find a way to operate a complex, expensive technological program, such as the space program, without giving up the openness and public debate that is characteristic of our democratic society? Nearly every phase of the U.S. space program reflects that conflict between the demands of an efficient technology and an open policy-making process.

4
EYES AND EARS IN SPACE

For most people around the world, *Sputnik* and *Explorer* were a real shock. Few had ever imagined the possibility of an artificial satellite circling the earth or thought about the potential value of such a device. But for a handful of scientists, *Sputnik* and *Explorer* were no great surprise. These scientists had been dreaming about, planning for, and testing artificial satellites for many years. Space scientists envisioned two general kinds of artificial satellites: scientific satellites and applications satellites.

Scientific satellites are those designed primarily to gather new information about the earth's atmosphere, our solar system, outer space, or the earth itself. Counting electrons in space, tracking the earth's magnetic field, and determining the precise shape of the earth are examples of measurements made by a scientific satellite. Applications satellites are those which have some specific practical value, such as transmitting messages, observing cloud patterns, or helping ships navigate.

Some satellites seem to belong in both categories. They collect new information at the same time that they carry out some practical function. The data relayed by a weather satellite, for example, can be used both to learn more about how weather systems develop and to predict tomorrow's weather.

In general, scientists use the term *scientific* when they refer to a satellite that is used solely to collect new data and is not also used for communication, navigation, weather forecasting, or some other specific, practical application.

U.S. POLICY ON SATELLITES

The National Aeronautics and Space Act of 1958 provided little specific guidance for a U.S. satellite program. The act did call for activities that would expand "human knowledge of phenomena in the atmosphere and space" and establish "long-range studies of the potential benefits to be gained from, the opportunities for, and the problems involved in the utilization of aeronautical and space activities." But the act said almost nothing about how these goals were to be achieved through specific programs.

A recent report by the Office of Technology Assessment points out that "the legislative mandate for NASA . . . has provided little guidance on the pace and content of the program. In some areas, notably space communications R&D and Earth resource systems, the act was of no use in resolving policy differences or in guiding executive branch action."[15]

In fact, most recommendations for scientific satellites have come from university scientists. Their suggestions for research projects have usually been channeled to NASA through the Space Sciences Board of the National Academy of Sciences.

Ideas for the earliest applications satellites, on the other hand, originated with private industry. Research for the first communications satellite system, for example, was initiated by American Telephone and Telegraph (AT&T). Had President Eisenhower had his way, that approach would have remained the policy of the U.S. government. He preferred to have private industry develop applications satellite systems, with government assistance only when and where necessary.

President Kennedy, however, wanted the government to take primary responsibility for *all* space programs, including all satellite systems. He believed that governmental control was necessary to ensure that the United States gained preeminence in all aspects of space research.

Kennedy saw the transfer of satellite systems to private industry as a later step in space technology. The problems associated with that transfer of satellite technology did not, as we will see, come easily, and even today, it is one of the most difficult issues in U.S. space policy.

U.S. SCIENTIFIC SATELLITES

Except for military launches, which constitute about 40 percent of all satellites put into orbit, most satellites are sent up to conduct scientific research.

Over the past thirty years, the United States and USSR have, between them, launched hundreds of scientific satellites. The possibilities for research by these satellites are staggering. Members of the U.S. Explorer series provide a hint of some of those possibilities.

After inheriting the Explorer program from the army in 1958, NASA launched forty-nine more satellites in this series. Some of the research carried out by these *Explorer*s included measuring atmospheric density at various altitudes above the earth, counting and tracking energetic particles, observing characteristics of planet earth, mapping and measuring the earth's magnetic field, and making astronomical observations from X-ray, gamma-ray, and radio sources in outer space.

Satellites have been especially valuable in astronomical research. Prior to 1957, almost everything we knew about our sun and moon, the planets, the stars, and interstellar space came from telescopic observations. That information was always limited by one unavoidable handicap: the earth's atmosphere.

Light or other forms of radiation collected by earth-based telescopes has to travel through the earth's atmosphere. And along that journey, some of that radiation is absorbed or dispersed by the atmosphere, reducing the amount that actually reaches telescopes. In addition, many forms of radiation—infrared, X-ray, gamma radiation, and ultraviolet light—penetrate the atmosphere hardly or not at all.

Telescopes traveling on satellites above the earth's atmosphere do not experience this problem. Therefore, astronomers have long looked forward to the day when they could send their telescopes into orbit on artificial satellites. Such earth-orbiting telescopes could be expected to be at least ten times more powerful than the largest optical telescope on earth. Orbiting Solar Observatory (OSO), Orbiting Astronomical Observatory (OAO), and High Energy Astronomy Observatory (HEAO) are three such U.S. astronomical/scientific programs.

Between 1962 and 1975, NASA rockets placed eight OSO satellites into orbit. Among the phenomena studied by these satellites were the number, pattern, and temperature of solar flares, X-ray and gamma-ray emissions from outer space, and cosmic rays within the earth's atmosphere. Three HEAO satellites were launched successfully between August 1977 and September 1979. The accomplishments of *HEAO 2,* the "Einstein observatory," were typical of those of its sister spacecraft. *HEAO 2* searched for and found many new X-ray sources in outer space; located new high-energy, galaxylike objects known as quasars and a new class of extremely hot stars known as O-stars; identified the oldest galaxies known to that date; tracked new pulsating stars (pulsars), neutron stars, and supernovae; and provided valuable new data on the origins of the universe.

SOVIET SCIENTIFIC SATELLITES

The names of most U.S. satellites suggest the purpose for which they were launched. For example, "Relay" satellites are used for communication, "Nimbus" for weather forecasting, and "Landsat" for earth surveys. But the same cannot be said for Soviet satellites. For whatever reason, the Soviets decided early on to designate a large number of their spaceflights with the name *Kosmos*. We now know that this name has been used for a great variety of flights: for military launches, for early tests of manned flight equipment, for failed missions, and for applications satellites (navigation; communication; weather-, land-, and ocean-surveying).

Many Kosmos flights have also carried scientific satellites into orbit. The missions of these Kosmos flights are similar to those of the Explorer, OSO, OAO, HEAO, and other U.S. scientific satellite programs.

The description of the launch of *Kosmos 1* by the Soviet newspaper *Tass* on March 16, 1962, is typical of hundreds of Kosmos launches made since that time. *Tass* claimed that the satellite would give "new means for studying the physics of the upper atmospheric layers and outer space." Specifically, *Kosmos 1* carried equipment that would allow it to carry out studies on

> the concentration of charged particles in the ionosphere for investigating the propagation of radio waves . . . corpuscular flows and low energy particles . . . the energy composition of the radiation dangers of prolonged space flights . . . the primary composition and intensity variation of cosmic rays . . . the magnetic field of the Earth . . . the short wave radiation of the sun and other celestial bodies . . . the upper layers of the atmosphere . . . the effects of meteoric matter on construction elements of space vehicles . . . and the distribution and formation of cloud patterns in the Earth's atmosphere.[16]

Many of the approximately eighteen hundred Kosmos flights launched to date have carried out scientific studies such as these.

In addition to Kosmos satellites, at least two Soviet series, Prognoz and Astron, parallel the U.S. astronomical satellite programs. The first Prognoz satellite was launched in April 1972, while the latest, *Prognoz 10,* went into orbit in April 1985. Like its U.S. cousins, the Prognoz satellites analyzed the earth's outer atmosphere, the composition and behavior of the sun, and the properties of outer space. Astron was apparently a short-lived project, launched on March 23, 1983, one of whose objectives was to listen for messages from intelligent civilizations outside our own solar system.

COMMUNICATION SATELLITES

The concept behind a communication satellite is simplicity itself. Imagine a large object—perhaps a big plastic balloon—in orbit above the earth. Radio signals generated at one point on the earth can be aimed at and bounced

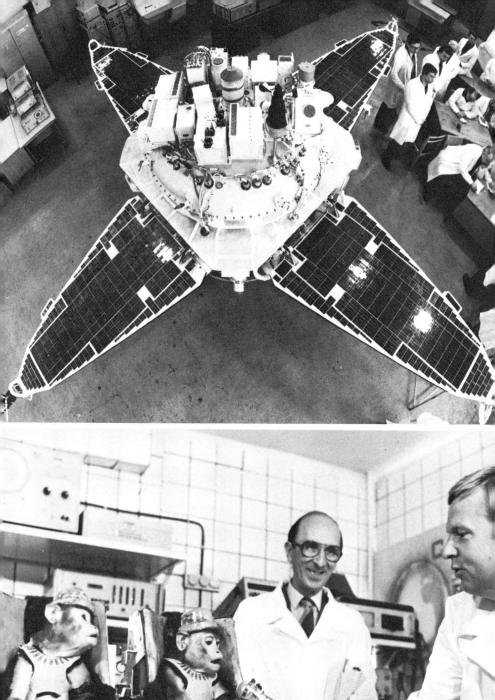

off that balloon. The reflected signals can then be picked up at some other distant point on the earth. Using this method, one can send messages from Phoenix to Rome, by way of outer space.

And, in fact, the method just described is that used in the first satellite-based communication system. *Echo 1* was nothing other than a large—30.5 m (101 ft) diameter—balloon made of mylar plastic sandwiched between two layers of aluminum foil. Folded into a compact package, the balloon was placed into orbit by a Thor-Delta rocket on August 12, 1960. Once in orbit, the package unfolded and inflated, and *Echo 1* assumed its full spherical shape. *Echo 2* joined its sister in orbit on January 25, 1964.

The Echo satellites are examples of *passive* communication satellites. They perform no other function than to be a target off which to bounce radio signals. A second type of satellite is said to be *active*. Instead of just reflecting radio waves, it "accepts" them. After receiving the message, it may relay (rebroadcast) the message immediately, amplify the message, or store the message and retransmit it at some later time.

Relay 1, launched on December 13, 1962, was NASA's first active communication satellite. It could accept and retransmit up to twelve simultaneous two-way telephone conversations or one television signal.

Both active and passive communication satellites orbit in "low altitudes" (a few hundred kilometers). A third kind of communication satellite travels in a very high orbit, at 35,880 km (22,300 mi). At this altitude, the speed at which the satellite travels around the earth exactly matches the speed at which the earth rotates on its axis. Thus, the satellite appears to remain motionless at a fixed point

Above: Prognoz 10 *(USSR)*
Below: *These Russian monkeys hold a press conference after their seven-day* Kosmos *flight in 1985.*

The trail of Echo 1 *(U.S.) is revealed through time-lapse photography.*

above the earth's surface. An observer viewing such a satellite would always see it in exactly the same place. Satellites of this kind are referred to as *geosynchronous* because their motion is *sync*hronized with that of the earth (*geo-*).

Geosynchronous satellites are especially valuable in communication because a set of three such satellites, located equidistant from each other in orbit, can provide coverage for the whole earth. The United States' first attempt at launching a geosynchronous satellite, *Syncom 1,* failed. However, *Syncom 2* and *Syncom 3* successfully reached orbit on July 26, 1963, and August 19, 1964.

Between 1966 and 1974 NASA launched six special communication satellites in the Applications Technology Satellite (ATS) series. The purpose of this series was to demonstrate how satellite technology could be applied to the solution of human problems. The accomplishments of the last in the series, *ATS-6,* illustrate the best features of that program.

A major feature of *ATS-6* was a 9-m (30-ft) antenna which could be pointed accurately at any part of the earth over which it passed. It was then able to relay signals from one part of the earth to another. In one experiment, specialists at the Veterans Administration, the University of Washington, and the University of Alaska provided medical and health information by way of the satellite to remote areas of Alaska where doctors are scarce. In another experiment, the government of India provided six hours of instruction daily for students in remote areas of the country where formal schooling was virtually nonexistent. *ATS-6* also had the capability to provide navigational information for airplanes and ships within reach of its orbit.

SOVIET COMMUNICATION SATELLITES

For reasons that are not entirely clear, the Soviet Union has lagged far behind the United States in most commercial satellite launchings. Certainly, with a land area that stretches more than 6,000 km (3,700 mi) from Leningrad to Vladivostok, the Soviets could use a reliable satellite communications system. Perhaps Soviet engineers simply took longer to develop the necessary electronic technology required for such a system. Or maybe the Soviet government chose to place its emphasis on other space activities, such as manned spaceflight.

In any case, the Soviets have trailed U.S. communication satellite development by, in most cases, at least three years. The first successful Soviet active repeater satellite, for example, was launched on April 23, 1965. This *Molniya 1* ("lightning") satellite was roughly comparable to the U.S. *Relay,* launched in late 1962.

As of this date, the Soviets are continuing to launch Molniya satellites to replace earlier models that, after a certain time in orbit, fall back into the earth's atmosphere and are destroyed. For example, *Molniya 3-24* (number twenty-four in the third class of Molniyas) was launched into orbit on May 29, 1985, to replace an earlier *Molniya,* number 3-l8.

Like the United States, the Soviets have developed more than one kind of communication satellite. The first of these satellite families, *Raduga* ("rainbow"), was launched in December 1975. It was later followed by *Ekran* ("screen," 1976), *Gorizont* ("horizon," 1978), *Loutch* ("beam," 1979), *Gals* ("tack," 1979), and *Volna* ("wave," 1980). All of these are, or will be, parts of geosynchronous communication systems.

PUBLIC VERSUS PRIVATE
OWNERSHIP OF SATELLITES

The early success of the U.S. communication satellite program was the source of great pride for NASA and the administration of President John F. Kennedy. But it also held the potential for some difficult political headaches for all involved.

No sooner had the practicability of communication satellites been demonstrated when questions began to arise about the management of this new technology: Should the operation of communication satellites continue to be a nonprofit governmental activity, or should it be turned over to private business? Should the United States maintain complete control of this "international" system, or should other nations be invited to join with us in its operation? Should efforts be made to prevent the communication system from falling into the hands of a giant monopoly (AT&T), or would that very event guarantee the most efficient operation of the system? (Of course, most of these questions would not arise in the Soviet Union.)

The congressional debate over these issues was one of the longest and most heated political disputes of any in the Space Age. Finally, on August 31, 1962, after twenty days of often bitter controversy, the Congress passed and President Kennedy signed the Communications Satellite Act of 1962. The act established the private Communications Satellite Corporation (Comsat), half of whose stock was to be held by the general public and half by communications industries (such as AT&T). Six Comsat directors were to be named by public stockholders, six by the communications industry, and three by the president. The board of directors was empowered and instructed to invite other nations to share in the investment, activities, expenses, and profits of the corporation.

The Comsat legislation was important not only because it resolved the potential problems created by NASA's successful satellite program, but also because it established a precedent in space research. Congress had agreed that technology produced and developed at public expense could then be released to private industry for exploitation and profit.

One of the first acts of Comsat's management was to initiate negotiations for an international communication system that could make use of its satellites. Again, the political problems involved in applying this technology were awesome. Since the United States obviously possessed nearly all of the technology and was responsible for a great majority of the world's communication business, it expected a major share of the control of any international system.

Under these circumstances, the Soviet Union and the Soviet bloc nations wanted nothing to do with a system they knew would be dominated by the United States. Other nations, while recognizing the present realities of the communications business, refused to accept a third-cousin role in the system.

By July 1964, however, the United States and fourteen other nations were able to resolve their differences. They joined to form the International Telecommunications Satellite Consortium (Intelsat). The United States maintained a dominant role in the policy making, operation, and financial affairs of the consortium, but it provided a mechanism by which other member nations might increase their share in the operation over time.

Less that nine months after the formation of Intelsat, Syncom placed its first satellite into orbit. Formally named *Intelsat 1*, the satellite was also widely known as *Early Bird 1*. This primitive (by today's standards) satellite could connect no more than two earth stations at one time via 240 circuits or one television channel. During its first year of operation, *Early Bird* carried a total of eighty hours of television broadcasting.

Over the past twenty years, both Intelsat and its satellite

systems have grown enormously. Today, 109 nations belong to the organization and have invested at least a billion dollars in its operation. By 1981, the sixteen satellites in orbit connected 976 earth stations with a capacity of 36,000 two-way circuits plus television channels. The system carried 35,658 hours of television in that year.

The Soviet bloc nations have established a joint communication program, similar to Intelsat, which they call Intersputnik. It was formed on November 15, 1971, when representatives from Bulgaria, Cuba, Czechoslovakia, East Germany, Hungary, Mongolia, Poland, Romania, and the Soviet Union agreed to the establishment of the Intersputnik system. The first transmissions on the Intersputnik system took place on November 7, 1973, with the telecast to Cuba of the Red Square parade in Moscow. At first, Intersputnik signals were transmitted exclusively on Molniya satellites. In later years, the system switched over first to Radugas and, finally and currently, to Gorizont satellites.

NAVIGATION SATELLITES
Probably the first suggestion ever made for a navigation satellite appeared in Edward Everett Hale's story "The Brick Moon," published in the *Atlantic Monthly* in 1869. Hale began by reviewing the navigation problem of ships at sea. They were usually out of sight of visible landmarks and had to find their location by using the stars. But stellar navigation is a lengthy process and cannot be used at all in bad weather or on cloudy nights. Hale suggested launching an artificial satellite about 200 ft in diameter into polar orbit around the earth. He pointed out that the satellite would be easily visible to ships at sea, who could use its known position to calculate their own.

The world's first navigational system, Transit, was designed to operate essentially like Hale's "Brick Moon." A ship at sea seeking its location would send out a radio signal to two Transit satellites. Both satellites would transmit this signal to a ground-based computer. The computer would then compare the two signals with each other. Knowing the position of the satellites and the difference between the two signals, the computer would then be able to calculate the ship's position. This information could then be transmitted from the computer back to a satellite and thence to the ship itself. With signals moving at the speed of light, the ship would know its position in virtually no time at all.

Unfortunately, the launch of the first satellite in the U.S. series, *Transit 1A*, on September 17, 1959, was unsuccessful. In fact, the early Transit program was plagued by launch problems, and only five of the first fourteen satellites reached their correct orbits and functioned properly. Not until June 4, 1964, then, could the system be declared operational.

Since 1964, the Department of Defense (DOD) has been the sponsor of the nation's navigational satellite system. It has successfully orbited more than a dozen Transit satellites as well as a more advanced navigational system known as Navstar.

SOVIET NAVIGATION SATELLITES

The Soviets began to talk about their own satellite navigational system as early as 1966. But they provided no specific information as to how the system operated or which satellites were involved. Their first version of the U.S. Transit satellite apparently reached orbit in 1967. The first definitive Soviet announcement of a navigational system did not appear, however, until March 31, 1978. On that date TASS News Agency reported that: "the *Kosmos 1000* satellite which was orbited on March 31 starts a new direction in the extensive utilization of space technology for the national economy. The specialty of [the] new satellite is sea navigation."[17]

The Soviets almost certainly had a navigation system in place much sooner than 1978, however, probably as early as 1962. All satellites that make up that (and later) systems carry the designation *Kosmos*, and the Soviets provide very little direct information about the systems.

Most of what we know about Soviet navigation satellites, therefore, comes from the analysis of satellite experts such as Nicholas L. Johnson at Teledyne Brown

Engineering Company and those working with the Kettering School group in Great Britain.

We believe that the present Soviet program consists of two navigational systems, called *Constellation 2* and *Constellation 3*. Each system consists of Kosmos satellites that orbit the earth about once every 105 minutes. The satellites in each system are placed into orbit in such a way that they cover all parts of the earth at one time. Thus, *Constellation 2* consists of six satellites whose orbits are separated by 30°, and *Constellation 3* contains four satellites whose orbits are separated by 45°. *Constellation 2* is intended for military uses, and *Constellation 3* for civilian uses. The Soviets, like their U. S. counterparts continuously replace satellites in all of their systems as the older machines fall into lower orbits and burn up as they reach the lower atmosphere.

WEATHER SATELLITES

Today's weather forecast is useful in helping us to decide whether or not to plan a picnic for tomorrow. But meteorology, the science of weather forecasting, has a great deal more economic value than picnic planning. Soviet officials estimate, for example, that their meteorological satellites save their economy more than a billion rubles (about $1.25 billion) every year by providing improved weather predictions for farmers and for air, ground, and water transportation systems, and about potentially disastrous storms.

Weather forecasting has long been handicapped by the complexity of factors that cause weather and by meteorologists' inability to get the "big picture" of those factors, primarily the movements of large air masses and fronts. But this is just the kind of task for which satellites are

Top: *U.S. satellite photograph of Hurricane Elena in 1985.* Bottom: *Soviet satellite photographs of cyclones.*

| 50 |

МОСКВА
(Moscow)

КИЕВ
(Kiev)

ideally suited. Traveling hundreds or thousands of kilometers above the earth's surface, weather satellites can observe large regions of the earth that could never be covered by weather planes or high-altitude balloons.

Little surprise, then, that the very first operational applications satellite was a weather satellite. *TIROS 1*, launched on April 1, 1960, was the first of a series of ten U.S. satellites with that name. All reached orbit between 1960 and 1965 and successfully transmitted optical and infrared photographs of the earth's cloud patterns. Although designed to last only a few months, all but *TIROS 1* greatly exceeded that prediction. *TIROS 8*, the most long-lived, produced data from orbit for 3½ years.

Since the TIROS program, the United States has put into operation even more sophisticated weather satellite systems: Nimbus (beginning in 1964); the TIROS Operational Satellite, or TOS (1966; name later changed to ESSA for Environmental Sciences Service Administration); Improved Tiros Operational Satellite, or ITOS (1970); and SM and GOES (1974; geosynchronous environmental satellites).

The Soviets also began early to test components of a weather satellite system. Kosmos flights in 1962 and 1963 carried electronic, optical, and mechanical equipment that would later be incorporated into their first operational satellite for meteorology, *Kosmos 122* (launched June 25, 1966). By 1969, the Soviets had deployed a full, operational system of weather satellites and assigned them the name Meteor. The Soviets continue to upgrade these satellites, having launched the first of thirteen "second-generation" *Meteor*s in 1975 and the first "third-generation" satellite in 1985.

EARTH RESOURCE SATELLITES

Any satellite equipped with a camera has the capability—whatever other mission it may have—of providing photographs of the earth's surface. Such photographs can be immensely valuable in helping scientists to assess a nation's land, water, mineral, and agricultural resources. With the proper kind of photographic equipment, a satellite can provide such diverse information as the best time to release livestock to a grazing area, the probable volume of timber that can be harvested in a forest, the location of schools of fishes, and the best place to look for new oil deposits. Some enthusiasts have classed the development of earth resource satellites with the discovery of fire or the invention of the wheel!

Remote sensing of earth resources is one area in which the Soviets seem clearly to have a more advanced program than the United States. The Soviet program makes use of three categories of space vehicles: recoverable satellites, manned spacecraft, and orbital satellites. All components of the remote earth-sensing system are now combined in the Soviet Priroda ("nature") program. (The term *Priroda* has been used for specific satellites, for a special mobile laboratory, for a data collection center, and for the earth resources program described below.)

Probably the first recoverable satellites used for earth resource studies were *Kosmos 210* and *214*, both of which stayed in orbit about a week. Launched in 1968, both satellites were primarily designed for military purposes. But they may well have collected photographs for earth resource assessment also. In succeeding years, Western specialists have identified many other Kosmos flights apparently designed for earth resource analysis also.

The Soviets have also used their manned spacecrafts and unmanned orbital stations to collect information about their natural resources. During its two years in orbit, for example, space station *Salyut 4* photographed more than 4.5 million sq km of Soviet land area. Earth photography was also an important object of certain manned flights, such as *Soyuz 9, 17,* and *22.* One Soviet expert claims that the information gained from the second of these flights saved the Soviet economy 50 million rubles (about $62 million).

The third element of the Priroda program is a set of Kosmos satellites in near-polar orbit. These satellites transmit photographs of the whole earth as it rotates below them. Current plans call for the launch of a new series of similar satellites beginning in 1986 "which will be able to carry out peaceful research into the land, sea, and atmosphere of the entire planet."[18]

LANDSAT

The "crown jewel" of the U.S. earth resource program is the Landsat series. Five satellites in this series were launched between July 23, 1972, and March 1, 1984. Each *Landsat* is designed to orbit the earth about once every 103 minutes, photographing a different 185-km-wide (115-mi-wide) strip as it moves north and south from pole to pole on each pass.

Photographs from *Landsat 1* and *2* were taken in four spectral (wavelength) bands; those from *Landsat 3, 4,* and *5,* in seven spectral bands, with resolution twice that of the earlier models. The *Landsat*s provided an enormous treasure of information about every portion of the earth. Their multicolor photographs (available to the public from the EROS Data Center in Sioux Falls, South Dakota)[19] have become familiar parts of many U.S. science books and magazines.

Like their communication satellite sisters, the *Landsat*s became highly valuable tools for commerce and industry. They relayed previously unavailable data about agriculture, mineral resources, urban development, land use, forestry, charting and mapping, water resource management, pollution control, earthquake prediction, and dozens of other geological and geographic topics.

The first *Landsat* was not in orbit long before private industries began to recognize its commercial potential. Discussions began almost immediately as to how soon and by what mechanisms operation of the Landsat system could be transferred from NASA to private commercial control. Echoing the earlier controversy about communication satellites, that debate has gone on in nearly every

Memphis, Tennessee, photographed by an American Landsat 4 *satellite. Can you identify the river?*

session of Congress since 1973. At least two dozen bills attempting to resolve the question have been introduced into the House and Senate. As of this date, none has yet been reported out of committee.

Presidents Carter and Reagan eventually transferred control of the Landsat system from NASA to the National Oceanographic and Atmospheric Administration (NOAA). However, the resolution of the longer-term question of the control and administration of the nation's earth resource sensing system still lies in the future.

5
A REVOLUTION IN ASTRONOMY

Pity the poor astronomer! Alone among scientists, astronomers for thousands of years were unable to examine and study the subjects of their interest firsthand. Unlike physicists, chemists, geologists, and biologists, astronomers could not go "into the field" to do research. Nor could they collect the objects of their study in a laboratory and do experiments on them. Instead, they had to depend on faint beams of light, radio waves, and those few other forms of radiation that earthbound telescopes manage to capture.

Pity the poor astronomer no more. Advances in space sciences since the 1950s have brought them the first really new tools they've had in hundreds of years: the satellite and the space probe. Using the same rockets that launch satellites and manned spacecraft, astronomers can now send highly automated and sophisticated measuring devices into space. These packages can be programmed to travel past ("fly by") a planet, go into orbit around the planet, or crash onto or land softly on the planet's surface. All the while, instruments on these space laboratories can send back information about their planetary target.

WATCHING FOR THE "WINDOW"

Planetary exploration was a major aspect of the early Soviet space program. The Soviets launched two probes toward Mars on October 10 and 14, 1960. In both cases, the plan was first to place the probe in orbit around the earth. Then the probe was to have been launched from its earth "parking" orbit on the second stage of its journey, a flyby of Mars.

Neither probe was successful even in reaching earth orbit. As is their custom, the Soviets never announced these failures. Outside observers determined much later, however, that the effort had been made . . . and failed.

One bit of evidence in this determination was the report that Premier Nikita Khrushchev had intended to announce the Mars probes during his visit to the United Nations in October 1960. A seaman who defected from Khrushchev's ship reported that a model of the Mars probe was on board with the premier. Khrushchev had apparently planned to display the model after the probe had reached Mars orbit successfully. Since the model was never shown in public, it may have returned to the Soviet Union with Premier Khrushchev.

One advantage that space detectives have in identifying Soviet planetary probes is the presence of launch "windows." A probe cannot be planned for a trip to Mars, Venus, or another planet at just any time. We can't hope to hit Mars, for example, if it's on the opposite side of the sun from the earth.

Launches are planned, then, for those times when earth and the target planet are relatively close to each other. Those best possible times for launch—"launch windows"—occur about every twenty-five months for Mars and every nineteen months for Venus.

A LONG DRY SPELL

Progress in planetary research in the five years following the two Mars probes was slow and discouraging. Both the United States and the USSR readied themselves for each Mars and Venus launch window. But both nations had to be satisfied with (at best) modest successes. It was a period when planetary scientists were learning a great deal about space technology, with relatively few concrete accomplishments to show for it.

For example, the first U.S. Mariner planetary probe, *Mariner 1*, flew off course at launch on July 22, 1962, and had to be destroyed. Its sister probe, *Mariner 2*, was launched successfully a month later. It traveled through interplanetary space for the next five months, continuously making measurements of its surrounding environment. Then, on December 13, *Mariner 2* made its closest pass, a not very near 34,853 km (21,657 mi), to Venus. The approach was not close enough to make really significant measurements of the planet. But the flight had become the first "near approach" to another planet.

The Soviet *Mars 1* probe of November 1, 1962 (they had failed to include their two 1960 failures in numbering their missions), became characteristic of a number of probes launched during this period. The probe reached earth orbit, left its parking orbit successfully, and reached its final destination . . . except that communications were lost somewhere along the way. Thus, the Soviets could report that *Mars 1 did* fly past Mars successfully at a distance of 193,000 km (120,000 mi). But they were unable to provide any new data about the Red Planet as a result of their "successful" flight. (Two other attempts during this launch window were never acknowledged by the Soviets because, although the probes reached earth orbit, they were unable to leave orbit and continue their journey to Mars.)

PROBES TO VENUS

Planned flights to Venus encountered similar problems. The Soviets' *Zond 1* (launched April 2, 1964) and *Venera 2* (November 12, 1965) both flew past the planet, and *Venera 3* (November 16, 1965) actually hard-landed on its surface. However, all three probes lost their telemetry systems along the way. Again, the Soviet "successes" produced no new data about our sister planet.

By 1967, both the U.S. and Soviet planetary programs appeared to be "on track," and our knowledge of Mars

and Venus began to grow by leaps and bounds. An important double success occurred in mid-October. The Soviets' *Venera 4* reached Venus, deployed a parachute, and dropped a capsule slowly through the planet's atmosphere. For an hour and a half, to an altitude of 25 km (15 mi) above the Venusian surface, the capsule transmitted the first-ever data from another planet, a temperature reading of 271°C (519°F) and a pressure of about twenty earth atmospheres.

One day later, the U.S. entry in the planetary race, *Mariner 5*, also reached Venus. With no plans to touch down, the U.S. probe flew by at a distance of 3,946 km (2,452 mi). As it passed, it collected an impressive amount of environmental data, including evidence for a weak magnetic field around the planet and a very dense atmosphere.

Venera 5 and *6* both reached the planet's surface in 1969, but severe conditions there prevented the telemetry system on both probes from returning any data. The first soft landing on Venus was achieved by *Venera 7* on December 15, 1971. A capsule designed to survive the high temperatures and pressures on Venus dropped from the probe itself and recorded temperatures of about 475°C (887°F) and pressures of about ninety atmospheres on the planet's surface. For nearly an hour, it transmitted these data—the first from another planet—to listening stations in the Soviet Union.

Venera 9 and *10* employed a new approach to planetary exploration. Each probe consisted of two parts, an orbiter and a soft-lander. Both Venera spacecraft reached Venus the same week in October 1975 and, upon arrival, separated into their two parts. The landers both reached the planet's surface without damage and transmitted the first television pictures from another planet. To the great surprise of earth observers, the Venusian cloud cover was less heavy than expected. In fact, the amount of light on

The Venusian probe
Mariner 2 *(U.S.)*

Top: *a model of the Soviet* Venera 9 *and* Venera 10 *Venus probes.* Bottom: *the Venusian surface as seen during the descent of* Venera 9 *in October 1975.*

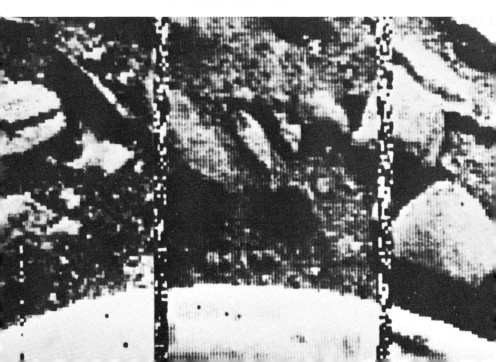

the planet's surface was about equal to that in Moscow on a cloudy day.

Meanwhile, the two Venera orbiters were studying the structure and temperature of the planet's atmospheres as well as the forms of radiation found there. They also served as a relay station for data coming from the landers.

THE U.S. "DOUBLE PLAY"

The next U.S. space probe to Venus *(Mariner 10)* included an extra touch. After sailing past Venus at a distance of 5,760 km (3,579 mi), the probe received an orbital correction and headed on toward the next innermost planet, Mercury. Seven weeks later, *Mariner 10* flew past Mercury and headed on toward the sun. After passing once around the sun, the probe passed Mercury a second time on September 21, 1974, and then once more on March 16, 1975. On its final flyby, *Mariner 10* passed within 327 km (203 mi) of the planet. The three hundred photos transmitted during this pass are the best—indeed, the only close-up—images we have of our sun's nearest neighbor.

The final two U.S. Venus probes, launched in 1978, received new names, *Pioneer Venus 1* and *2*. The first of these spacecraft was designed to orbit the planet for at least eight months in a gradually decreasing orbit. As it spiraled ever downward, it measured dozens of atmospheric properties and mapped part of the planet's surface.

Pioneer Venus 2 consisted of five parts: one large probe, three smaller probes, and the "bus" that carried the whole package. After reaching the planet, the *Pioneer Venus 2* bus released the four probes, which returned data on the Venusian atmosphere before crashing on the planet's surface.

SOVIET PROBES TO MARS

The gradually more complex approach to studying Venus—flyby, hard landing, soft landing, and orbiter—was also employed in probes to Mars. After its initial not too near miss with *Mars 1* in 1962, the Soviets waited nearly ten years before resuming an even minimally successful program of Mars probes.

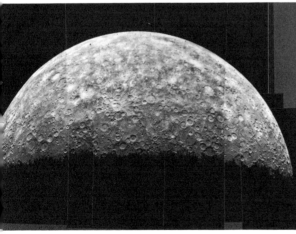

Top: *Venus seen from* Mariner 10
Bottom: Mariner 10 *photographs of Mercury*

The next two Mars probes were designated as *Zond 2* and *Zond 3*. *Zond 1*, you may recall, was the name given to a 1964 Venus mission. The name was also used for the test of equipment used in unmanned lunar flights from 1968 to 1973 (*Zonds 4* through *8*). *Zond 2* passed within 1,500 km (932 mi) of Mars, while *Zond 3* was launched outside a launch window and failed to pass near the planet.

When this program did resume, it was plagued by a series of failures and disappointments. Of the last six officially designated "Mars" flights, two were complete failures, and three, partial failures. In addition, Western experts believe that other probable Mars efforts were given Kosmos designations when they failed.

All Mars flights after *Mars 1* were combinations of or-biters and landers. In the case of *Mars 2* and *3*, each spacecraft carried both components in a single package. In the case of the last four probes, the orbiters (*Mars 4* and *5*) were matched with, but launched separately from, the landers (*Mars 6* and *7*).

Neither *Mars 2* nor *Mars 3* was very successful. In both cases, the orbiters attained Mars orbit and transmitted atmospheric and surface data about the planet. But both landers appear to have been destroyed or damaged either during landing or shortly thereafter.

Of the last four Mars spacecrafts: *Mars 4* failed to reach orbit and flew by at a distance of 2,000 km (1,200 mi); *Mars 5* did achieve orbit and functioned as planned; *Mars 6* transmitted a signal during 148 seconds of its descent to the planet's surface, but then was lost; and a rocket on *Mars 7* malfunctioned and the spacecraft missed the planet by 1,300 km (830 mi).

The Soviets are currently planning to launch two more vehicles towards Mars in July 1988. The mission is code-named Phobos-88. The plan is to first orbit both vehicles around Mars. Then, one orbit will be modified so that one vehicle goes into orbit around the planet's moon, Phobos. The plan is to bring the spacecraft to within 50 m (160 ft) of the moon's surface. If all goes well, the second orbit will also be changed so that the other spacecraft will be placed into near orbit around Mars's second moon, Dei-mos.

THE U.S. MARS PROGRAM

The U.S. Mars program has been more successful than that of the Soviets and more impressive than its own Venus program. Five years after the flyby of *Mariner 4*, sister ships *Mariner 6* and *7* were launched on similar missions. They also passed the planet, at distances of 3,200 km (2,000 mi) and 3,500 km (2,200 mi), returning photographs of about 10 percent of the Martian surface.

By far the most spectacular U.S. achievements, however, were those of *Mariner 9* and *Viking 1* and *2*. The last two Mars *Mariners* were designed to go into orbit around the planet and obtain the most detailed photographs yet seen of Mars. Although *Mariner 8* did not survive launch, its companion probe, *Mariner 9*, did achieve Martian orbit on November 10, 1971.

Space scientists were at first discouraged by the photos returned from Mars. For two months, the planet was covered by a gigantic dust storm. But, by early 1972, the storms had subsided and the spacecraft was able eventually to photograph 85 percent of the planet's surface as well as its two moons, Phobos and Deimos.

The U.S. agenda for 1975 was similar to the Soviet plan of four years earlier. Two spacecraft, named *Viking 1* and *2*, were each to contain two parts, an orbiter and a lander. The orbiters were to take pictures of Mars from space, measure the amount of water vapor in the Martian atmosphere, monitor temperatures on the planet's surface, and act as a relay station for signals from the landers. The landers, in turn, were highly complex machines with many tasks: "listening" for Marsquakes, studying the planet's lower atmosphere, photographing the surface area around the lander, and analyzing the Martian soil.

The last assignment was perhaps the most intriguing. Each lander had a retractable claw which could reach out,

Top: Viking 2 (U.S.) photograph of the surface of Mars. Bottom: a working model of the Viking lander.

scoop up a soil sample, and deliver the sample to an automated chemical laboratory in the lander. This analysis was designed not only to determine the physical and chemical composition of the soil, but also to determine whether forms of life did then exist, or ever had existed, on the planet.

Viking 1 arrived in Mars orbit on June 19, 1976, and *Viking 2* on August 7, 1976. Both landers reached the planet's surface successfully, and they and the orbiters continued to relay data until Mars passed behind the sun in November 1976. A month later, Mars reappeared on the other side of the sun, and both landers and orbiters began transmitting data again. Although scientists expected the landers to last only a year or two, both were still transmitting data about four years later, *Lander 2* until April 1980 and *Lander 1* until November 1982.

The most interesting question of all—as to the presence of life on Mars—was not answered to everyone's satisfaction. While no positive evidence of life was found, some experimental results were ambiguous, indicating that the existence of some life forms at some time in the past was not completely impossible. Scientists look forward to the day when a more sophisticated Mars probe may be able to give a really positive answer to this intriguing puzzle.

PIONEER AND *VOYAGER* TO THE OUTER PLANETS

By the early 1970s, U.S. space scientists had begun to turn their attention to the outer planets, particularly Jupiter and Saturn. Two space probes, designated *Pioneer 10* and *11*, were launched on March 3, 1972, and April 6, 1973, with the highest velocities ever given a rocket, more than 50,000 km/hr (31,000 mi/hr). During its twenty-one-month, 992-million-km (616-million-mi) journey to Jupiter, *Pioneer 10* passed beyond the orbit of Mars, through the asteroid belt, finally passing within 129,000 km (80,000 mi) of our solar system's largest planet.

While passing Jupiter, *Pioneer 10* transmitted data on the planet's surface features, its atmosphere, and its famous Red Spot. After the Jupiter encounter, *Pioneer 10* continued outward from the sun, passing the orbits of Saturn, Uranus, and Neptune. In 1987 it also passed through Pluto's orbit, making it the first human-made object to leave the solar system.

By December 1970, *Pioneer 11* had repeated her sister probe's trip to Jupiter. This trip was programmed, however, to bring the spacecraft within 42,000 km (26,000 mi) of the planet. This trajectory not only allowed *Pioneer 11* to take much better photographs of Jupiter and its satellites, but also made it possible to use the giant planet's gravitational attraction to swing the probe around Jupiter and, like a slingshot, aim it toward Saturn. Nearly five years later, *Pioneer 11* passed through the rings and within 21,400 km (13,300 mi) of our second largest planet. After this pass, the spacecraft also headed toward outer space.

Attached to both *Pioneer 10* and *11* is a plaque depicting a man and a woman, a diagram of our solar system, and some additional information about the probe's earthbound inhabitants. The plaque is intended as a message of greeting to any intelligent being with whom the probes might ever come into contact in outer space.

While planning for the *Mariner 10* flyby of Venus and Mercury in 1973, NASA scientists realized that an unusual opportunity awaited them late in the decade. At that time, all five outer planets—Jupiter, Saturn, Uranus, Neptune, and Pluto—would be aligned in a very special way. The last such alignment had occurred during the presidency of Thomas Jefferson, and a similar opportunity would not be available until about the year 2150.

When the planets assume this configuration, a single earth spacecraft is capable of flying by all five on a single flight. Although the U.S. Congress decided not to fund the complete "Grand Tour" of the planets suggested by NASA, it did approve a modified version of that project, to be carried out by *Voyager 1* and *2*.

Under this program, the two spacecraft were launched on August 20, 1977 (*Voyager 2*) and September 5, 1977 (*Voyager 1*). Because they traveled along slightly different paths, *Voyager 1* actually arrived at Jupiter four months

Top: *scale model of* Voyager *(U.S.)*
Bottom: *Saturn, photographed by* Voyager 1

Top: Voyager 1 *closeup of surface of Jupiter* Bottom:
Voyager 2 *shot of Uranus, showing one of its rings*

earlier than its sister probe, on March 5, 1979. After observing the planet and its satellites, both probes flew on to Saturn, from which they returned spectacular photos of the planet, its mysterious rings, and its satellites.

After passing Saturn, *Voyager 1* headed into outer space to join its cousins, *Pioneer 10* and *11*. Similar to the greetings carried on the *Pioneers*, both *Voyager 1* and *2* carry a "Sounds of Earth" record. The recording contains two hours of music and sounds and digitally recorded data carrying pictures and a spoken greeting from President Jimmy Carter.

Voyager 2 had two more assignments before it left the solar system: rendezvous with Uranus and Neptune. The first of those two challenges was met in January 1986 when the spacecraft returned unusually clear and informative pictures of a planet that, until then, we had barely understood. *Voyager 2* continues on its second mission, a 1989 meeting with the solar system's next-to-last planet, Neptune.

6

DESTINATION: THE MOON

Humans have dreamed for centuries of traveling to the moon. Perhaps the first science fiction story of all time was Lucian of Samosata's *A True History,* written in the second century A.D. Lucian's storyteller sets sail from the Straits of Gibraltar into that terrible expanse of the unknown, the Atlantic Ocean. Caught in a storm, he is carried off to the moon, where a war is going on between residents of the sun and those of the moon.

One of history's great astronomers, Johannes Kepler, also wrote about a fanciful trip to the moon. In *Somnium,* published in 1634, after his death, Kepler described the moon as he thought it to exist: an intensely hot moon day equal in length to fourteen earth days followed by an equal period of freezingly cold nights.

Writers have imagined a dazzling variety of ways by which humans might reach the moon: by flying with one wing of a vulture and one of an eagle (in Lucian's second moon tale, *Icaromenippus*); riding in Elijah's chariot (Ariosto's *Orlando Furioso*, in 1532); floating on a raft pulled by swanlike birds (Francis Godwin's *A Man in the Moon*, in 1638); being pulled upward by phials of dew or enormous jumps of a mechanical grasshopper (Edmond Rostand's *Cyrano de Bergerac,* in 1897); or exploding

upward from the mouth of a giant cannon (Jules Verne's *From the Earth to the Moon*, in 1865). In contrast to these glorious visits, the first actual flights to the moon in the 1960s seem almost a bit mundane!

BEGINNINGS OF THE
U.S. LUNAR PROGRAM

The early history of the U.S. space program was marked by disagreement among experts as to whether this nation's moon program should aim at placing a human on the moon (a manned flight) or whether lunar exploration could be done as well by automated equipment (unmanned flight). Although the Soviets do not share with us the disagreements that must take place in their planning of space policy, we presume that similar arguments must have occurred in Moscow.

Suffice to say here that the first steps in any moon program, manned or unmanned, are much the same. One begins by flying probes past the moon, then putting them into orbit around the moon, then crashing them on the moon, and finally dropping them gently on the surface of the moon.

If a human is to ride along in stages two and four, a way must be devised to get the person safely back to earth. That means having a larger spacecraft and a more powerful rocket to carry it into space. Otherwise, the technology of manned and unmanned flight is similar in many ways.

The U.S. apparently had an early lead in moon flights. Our Pioneer program launched its first probe to the moon only ten months after *Sputnik 1* reached orbit. Unfortunately, the spacecraft (later named *Pioneer 0*) flew for only seventy-seven seconds before the launch vehicle exploded. Three more efforts, *Pioneers 1, 2,* and *3*, experienced similar failures in October, November, and De-

An illustration from an
edition of Jules Verne's
From the Earth to the Moon

cember of 1958. The next flight, *Pioneer 4,* was more successful. Launched on March 3, 1959, *Pioneer 4* passed within 60,000 km (37,000 mi) of the moon before going into orbit around the sun. The next three *Pioneers* were again failures as rockets failed or blew up before leaving the earth's atmosphere.

THE SOVIET LUNA PROGRAM

Although starting somewhat later, the Soviets found success before the United States. Their *Luna 1,* launched on January 2, 1959, was intended to strike the moon. It barely missed on that mission, but did pass within 6,000 km (3,700 mi) of the moon's surface. *Luna 2* was more successful, striking the moon's surface on September 13, 1959. It returned no data about the moon, however. *Luna 3* was a spectacular success for the Soviets. Launched on October 4, 1959, it flew past the moon at a distance of 7,000 km (4,300 mi), returning pictures of its never-before-seen far side.

After *Luna 3,* the Soviets made no announced moon flights for more than three years. During this time, they were developing a second generation of moon probes. The first-generation probes (*Lunas 1* through *3*) had been launched directly from the earth to the vicinity of the moon. An extremely powerful rocket is needed to propel a probe all that distance. And that is one feature of space technology that the Soviets have never been very successful in developing.

By 1963, the Soviets were ready to test another method for getting spacecraft to the moon. Second-generation *Lunas* (*Lunas 4* through *14*) were placed first in an earth orbit, then fired from this parking orbit toward the moon. This approach does not require as powerful a launch rocket as did *Lunas 1* through *3*. The purpose of the second-generation Luna probes was to land a spacecraft safely on the moon, from where it was to return data to the earth. None of the first six second-generation probes was successful. One failed to leave earth orbit, two flew past the moon, and three crashed on the moon's surface and were destroyed.

Then, on February 3, 1966 . . . success! *Luna 9* landed softly on the moon (the first human machine to do so) and began recording and transmitting television and radio signals. *Lunas 10* through *14* were also successful, each attaining lunar orbit or landing softly on the moon. The Soviets ended this phase of their moon program in 1968.

U.S. *RANGERS, SURVEYORS,* AND *LUNAR ORBITERS*

Meanwhile, the U.S. moon program appeared to be stuck in neutral gear. Having given up on the disastrous Pioneer series in the late 1960s, the United States placed its hopes on a new program, code-named Ranger. Again, disappointment was the order of the day. The first six Ranger probes all failed to leave the earth's atmosphere, missed the moon by a wide mark, or, in one case, crashed on the far side of the moon. By summer 1964, after fourteen consecutive failures, U.S. space scientists were under enormous pressure to produce a winner . . . and soon!

That winner was *Ranger 7,* launched on July 28, 1964. Designed to fly very close to the moon, the probe returned 4,304 excellent, high-resolution pictures of the moon's Sea of Clouds. Its sister probes, *Ranger 8* and *9,* repeated that success, transmitting, respectively, 7,137 photos of the Sea of Tranquility and 5,814 photos of the region around Crater Alphonsus. By mid-1965, the U.S. flyby program had finally accomplished its long-frustrated mission.

The next stage in the U.S. lunar program was similar to that of the second-generation Luna flights: to soft-land observational and measuring devices on the moon, and to place similar spacecraft into orbit around the moon. Five of the seven Surveyor flights designed to land on the moon and all five Lunar Orbiter missions were completely successful.

Between May 30, 1966, and January 7, 1968, the five *Surveyors* took nearly seventy thousand photographs of the moon's surface. In addition, *Surveyor 3* and *4* included a device for digging into the lunar soil and photographing the underlying material.

Surveyor 6 added one other twist to its other missions: It fired its rockets, lifted a few meters off the lunar surface, and moved to a new position 2.5 m (2.8 yd) away. The most advanced members of the Surveyor team, numbers 5, 6, and 7, also carried equipment for analyzing the chemical composition of the lunar soil.

Although the *Lunar Orbiter*s carried out measurements on the region above the moon's surface, their primary function was to photograph potential landing sites for a manned spacecraft. The five *Orbiter*s produced a total of 1,004 photographs for this purpose. The programmed crash of *Lunar Orbiter 5* on the moon on January 31, 1968, brought to an end the United States' unmanned moon program. After this date, all U.S. spacecraft to the moon have carried humans.

SOVIET LUNAR FLIGHTS SINCE 1969
The Soviets, on the other hand, have continued unmanned exploration of the moon beyond the U.S. Surveyor and Orbiter programs and into the third generation of their own Luna series. The final (to date) phase of the Soviet program was initiated on July 13, 1969, with the launch of *Luna 15*. The flight of this probe was, until quite recently, an intriguing mystery to U.S. observers. It was scheduled to reach lunar orbit just two days prior to the arrival of U.S. *Apollo 11,* the first scheduled landing of humans on the moon's surface.

Most observers felt that the Soviets intended to soft-land *Luna 15* on the moon, automatically remove a sample of lunar soil, and then return that sample in *Luna 15* to earth. If that was the Soviet plan, it failed when *Luna 15* crashed on the moon and was unable to complete its mission.

Succeeding third-generation flights were much more impressive. *Luna 16,* for example, achieved the presumed *Luna 15* mission, returning a 101-g (3.5-oz) sample of lunar soil on September 24, 1970. And *Luna 17* carried with it the first mobile vehicle to reach the moon's surface. This *Lunokhod* moon buggy looked like a very large kettle with eight wheels (four on either side). The vehicle could

The Lunokhod 1 *moon buggy (USSR)*

be driven across the lunar terrain by means of signals from the earth.

During its ten months of operation on the moon, *Lunokhod 1* traveled a total of 10.54 km (6.549 mi), took more than twenty thousand television pictures, conducted soil tests, and made a number of astronomical observations. *Luna 20* and *24* repeated the soil sample returns of *Luna 16,* while *Luna 21* carried a second *Lunokhod* to the moon. The 1976 *Luna 24* flight was the last of this series of Soviet third-generation moon probes.

In 1985, the USSR announced the next stage in its unmanned exploration of the moon. Planned for a 1989 or 1990 launch, the latest third-generation *Luna*s will fly in a polar orbit around the moon. Their purpose will be to collect further information about the moon's surface and environment and to select locations for future soil-return missions.

7
HUMANS IN SPACE

For many people, manned spaceflights *are* a nation's space program. No matter how much commercial satellites may contribute to our standard of living or how much we can learn from planetary probes, spacecraft that carry men and women into earth orbit, to the moon, or beyond may still seem to be the ultimate aim of U.S. and Soviet space programs.

Certainly space scientists in both countries began early on to prepare for manned spaceflights. Between 1946 and 1952, for example, the Soviets claim to have launched eighteen vertical rockets carrying twelve different animals (usually dogs) to altitudes as great at 96 km (60 mi). On one occasion in May 1957, a single rocket carried five dogs to an altitude of 211 km (131 mi). The climax of this program in late 1957 was the launch of *Sputnik 2,* with its canine cosmonaut, Laika, the first living animal to travel in orbit around the earth.

American researchers were also using high-altitude balloons and ballistic rockets to test the effects of spaceflight on animals, usually monkeys and chimpanzees. In December 1959, for example, as part of the U.S. Mercury Project, a rhesus monkey named Sam traveled on a Little Joe rocket to an altitude of 85 km (53 mi). Two months later, on a 666-km (414-mi), 16.5-minute suborbital flight, the chimpanzee Ham tested the Mercury capsule whose next occupant would be the United States' first man in space, Alan Shepard.

MANNED SPACEFLIGHTS
AND POLITICS

Why send humans into space? That question has been the source of great debate for nearly forty years. Certainly, many space experiments can be done nearly as well by automated machines as they can by humans. And unmanned flights do not present the problems of ensuring human safety. The Soviet Venera probes and Lunokhod vehicles and the U.S. Viking and Surveyor spacecraft have demonstrated this point.

Of course, machines can never work as effectively as humans in a new environment. The U.S. Apollo program demonstrated the advantages of having humans present to make decisions, unexpected observations, and new plans when circumstances required these skills.

At least one factor in this continuing manned-versus-unmanned debate is the political advantage that comes from a successful manned space program. For example, the early years of the Soviet space program can best be understood in light of the prestige it brought to the USSR in general and, more specifically, to Premier Nikita Khrushchev.

As mentioned earlier, the launch of *Sputnik 1* was as much a political event as it was a scientific achievement. In fact, assessed on purely scientific criteria, the earliest U.S. satellites were probably superior to their Soviet counterparts. What really mattered to the general public, however, was that *Sputnik* was *first*.

Premier Khrushchev recognized this point. He realized early on the propaganda value of a successful Soviet manned space program. In fact, many events in the young Soviet space program make little sense unless examined in this light.

To a space scientist, a manned space program should consist of a series of incremental steps. At each stage, gradually more complex equipment is tested. Humans are never asked to fly until engineers are as certain as they can be that the equipment is safe. This agenda describes the U.S. Mercury, Gemini, and Apollo manned space programs. It probably also describes the program that the Soviets' leading space scientist, Sergei Korolev, would have preferred to follow. But Korolev worked in a difficult atmosphere. For sixteen years, under the reign of Joseph Stalin, he had been in various Soviet prisons. After Stalin's death in 1956, he was restored to favor and rapidly developed a promising relationship with the new Soviet ruler, Nikita Khrushchev.

In many ways, Korolev and Krushchev had similar aims: advancing the Soviet space program. However, Korolev was more concerned with scientific and technological progress, while Khrushchev saw the space program as a powerful propaganda tool. Thus, from time to time, Korolev's scientific agenda was forced to yield to the premier's political demands. As one writer has said,

Yuri Gagarin (left) and Sergei Korolev, after Gagarin's historic flight in Vostok 1 *on April 12, 1961*

Khrushchev had a very precise idea of what he was spending money on space shots for: to create the image, both at home and abroad, of a powerful Soviet technology and a progressive and efficient Khrushchev regime. . . .

Space research did not interest him. . . . Following the success of each project, Khrushchev ordered the cancellation of follow-on launchings of the same type, which, while promising to be more scientifically productive, would only appear to be "repetitious" and would not result in new gasps of shock and fear around the world.

. . . Since Khrushchev controlled the purse strings, it was Korolev who accommodated himself to the political demands.[20]

The stunning accomplishments of Korolev's manned Vostok and Voskhod programs, for which Khrushchev took full credit, must be analyzed, therefore, not only in scientific, but also in political, terms.

A STRING OF "FIRSTS"

Those accomplishments began on April 12, 1961, when Major Yuri Alekseyevich Gagarin, aboard *Vostok 1,* became the first human to orbit the earth. *Vostok* (which means "East") was launched from the Tyuratum cosmodrome, stayed in orbit for 108 minutes, and returned to earth in Kazakhstan. Gagarin's capsule completed its journey when a parachute deployed in the lower atmosphere, floating the spacecraft and its cosmonaut to a soft landing on Soviet soil.

News of Gagarin's flight produced many of the same shock waves in the United States and around the world as those of *Sputnik 1* four years earlier. Newspapers in the Third World, for example, saw the flight as evidence that the "U.S. is losing the space race with Russia" and hailed the Soviet feat as more important than the invention of the printing press (from Tunisia) or the discovery of the New World (from Iran) or of the wheel (from Kenya).[21]

Some observers believe that the timing of Major Ger-

Top: *Gagarin's homecoming in Moscow*

man Titov's flight on *Vostok 2* had some political significance also. His flight on August 6, 1961, came at nearly the same time as the building of the Berlin Wall. Premier Khrushchev may have felt the need for some positive propaganda at a time when world reaction to Soviet policy was otherwise less than enthusiastic.

In any case, the flight of *Vostok 2* had not made U.S. space scientists any more comfortable. By this date they still had only two suborbital manned flights (*Mercury 3* and *4*) to their credit. But it was the flights of *Vostok 3* and *4* that initiated a number of Soviet missions which, while spectacular, sometimes carried a bit of the bizarre about them.

Vostok 3 and *4* were launched one day apart, on August 11 and 12, 1962. Once in space, the two crafts came within visible range—6.5 km (4.0 mi)—of each other. The flights showed a high degree of accuracy in Soviet space

Premier Nikita Khrushchev and
President John F. Kennedy

navigation and a surprisingly rapid ability to prepare and launch the second *Vostok*.

In June of 1963, Lt. Col. Valeriy Bykovskiy set a space endurance record in *Vostok 5* (119 hr, 6 min) that would last for six years.

The final Vostok flight, *Vostok 6,* was of interest for two reasons. First, it was the first flight of a woman, Valentina Tereshkova, in space. Launched only two days after *Vostok 5,* Ms. Tereshkova simply rode in her space capsule for three days. (At that point, she had spent more time in space than all six Mercury astronauts together.)

That's the second interesting point about this flight. The sole purpose of *Vostok 6* appears to have been to place *a woman* into space. No new technology was used, and no aspect of the flight was any different from earlier *Vostok*s. From a scientific standpoint, there seems to have been no reason for the flight. But from a political standpoint, *Vostok 6* made a great deal of sense.

Ms. Tereshkova was hardly a typical cosmonaut candidate. When recruited for the space program, she was a worker in a textile factory. Her primary qualification may have been her interest in sport parachuting. In fact, the main reason she was selected may have been that she had *no* special qualifications.

Premier Khrushchev was eager to show the world that Soviet scientists had been so successful that spaceflight had become routine. Anyone could, with a minimal amount of training, travel in orbit around the earth.

After her *Vostok 6* experience, Ms. Tereshkova never flew again. Instead, she became the official Soviet spokesperson for the role of women in Soviet society. In a typical review of her experience, she pointed out that: "Since 1917 Soviet women have had the same prerogatives and rights as men. They share the same tasks. They are workers, navigators, chemists, aviators, engineers. And now the nation has selected me for the honor of being a cosmonaut. As you can see, on earth, at sea, and in the sky, Soviet women are the equal of men."[22]

Dramatic and serious, or frivolous and possibly hazardous, Ms. Tereshkova's flight may have been. The fact is that, for whatever reason, it would be another twenty years before an American woman would travel in space.

SCIENCE VERSUS POLITICS:
THE VOSKHOD PROGRAM

The next logical step in the Soviet space program was apparent to any space researcher. Korolev's one-person Vostok spacecraft had performed well (even given the Khrushchevian sideshow along the way). Clearly, the next spacecraft should be a two-person craft. And that, indeed, was Korolev's plan. The only problem was that the two-person *Soyuz* he was designing would not be ready for at least two years . . . and Premier Khrushchev had an important political goal to meet long before then.

For the two-man U.S. Gemini program was due to get underway in early 1965. The Soviets could scarcely allow the "backward" Americans to move ahead of them in the space race. The obvious next step in the "propaganda" race, then, was for the Soviets to launch a *three*-person space vehicle before the first Gemini flight. Consequently, Premier Khrushchev ordered Korolev to modify the one-person Vostok to allow it to carry three cosmonauts!

Such a plan was highly dangerous. The Vostok could be made to hold three passengers only by cutting safety provisions to a bare minimum. The safety ejection seat was removed, and only enough food and water for one day's flight was provided. Even then, space was so limited inside the capsule that the cosmonauts could not wear space suits. (The disastrous consequences of this decision became obvious in the flight of *Soyuz 11,* eight years later.) The plan was to get the space travelers up, take them in a few orbits around the earth, and then, with fingers still crossed, land them safely.

The refitted and renamed *Voskhod* (or "rising") *1* took off on October 12, 1964, and returned to earth twenty-four hours later. Ironically, during that short flight, Premier Khrushchev was removed from office. The courageous cosmonauts in *Voskhod 1* were greeted on their return by the new Soviet leaders, Leonid Brezhnev and Aleksei Kosygin.

In spite of Premier Khrushchev's ouster, a second (and final) *Voskhod* was launched on March 18, 1965. The aim of this mission was to allow the first ever extravehicular activity (EVA), or "space walk." Cosmonaut Aleksei Leonov was able to complete that mission . . . but just barely. He was returned to the spacecraft only with the greatest exertion.

Then, so much time had been spent on the walk that the Voskhod capsule fell behind in its normal flight plan and landed more than 3,000 km (2,000 mi) off course. Instead of stepping out onto the flat steppes of Kazakhstan, Leonid and his partner Pavel Belyayev found themselves in the midst of a fierce snowstorm in the Ural Mountains.

The Soviets had racked up another of their space spectaculars, the first space walk. But much had gone wrong during the flight of *Voskhod 2*. If the Soviets had not already decided to reassess the progress of their manned spaceflight program, this last of Premier Khrushchev's space follies could have made them do so!

"BEFORE THE END OF THIS DECADE"

The Soviets hold no monopoly on the political uses of space. The United States' young space program was just getting under way during a crucial turning point in American history. John F. Kennedy was elected president in 1960 with a pledge to "get the nation moving again." Some observers saw Kennedy's election as a watershed between the staid, conservative politics of the "tired old warrior," Dwight Eisenhower, and the beginning of a New Camelot under the fresh, young Kennedy.

And space research was not an insignificant factor in Kennedy's election. In fact, one of his telling campaign themes had been the "missile gap" which Eisenhower had (supposedly) allowed to open between the United States and the USSR. Some of Kennedy's advisers saw the space program as an entirely logical place for the new administration to push forward. A report from the President's Space Science Board recommended in 1961 a vigorous manned space program because of "the sense of national leadership [that would emerge] from bold and imaginative U.S. space activity." The Board went on to argue that "man's exploration of the Moon and planets [is] potentially the greatest inspirational venture of this century and one in which the whole world can share; inherent here are great and fundamental philosophical and spiritual values which find a response in man's questing spirit and his intellectual self-realization."[23]

By early 1961, the dramatic possibilities of space must have become increasingly appealing to a stumbling Kennedy administration. On April 12, Yuri Gagarin had become the first human in space, a bitter disappointment for U.S. scientists. And, closer to home, the president had suffered a disastrous political defeat in the abortive invasion of Cuba at the Bay of Pigs.

In this context, it's easy to see the appeal that a bold new attack on space might have for Kennedy. It would at the same time put the United States in an aggressive position in the race with the Soviets for space dominance, distract attention from the invasion fiasco in Cuba, and provide a new vision for the U.S. public.

At a joint session of Congress on May 25, 1961, President Kennedy challenged the assembled lawmakers and the general public with a new goal for the U.S. space program: "I believe that this nation should commit itself to achieving the goal, before this decade is out, of landing a man on the moon and returning him safely to the earth. No single space project in this period will be more impressive to mankind, or more important for the long-range exploration of space; and none will be so difficult or expensive to accomplish."[24]

The president had not misjudged the probable effects of his proposal. Support from Congress, the media, and the general public poured in. NASA's appropriations jumped from $964 million in 1961 to $1.83 billion in 1962, $3.67 billion in 1963, and $5.1 billion in 1964.

NASA was delighted, if a bit overwhelmed, by its new mission. The existing Mercury program was relatively modest, and not everyone at the space agency was sure that it could intelligently spend all the money being thrown at it. And the challenge of putting humans on the moon within nine years was terrifying. Most U.S. space scientists had viewed that as a reasonable goal for the mid-1970s!

MERCURY LEADS TO GEMINI

The die was cast. Within months, the United States' sometimes-on, sometimes-off space program had shifted into high gear. Following Alan Shepard's first suborbital flight on May 5, 1961, NASA's Project Mercury produced a string of uninterrupted successes: John Glenn's first orbital flight, and three-, six-, and twenty-two-orbit flights by Scott Carpenter, Wally Schirra, and Gordon Cooper. At the conclusion of Cooper's flight in May 1963 (one month before the final Vostok launch), the Mercury program was declared a complete success.

The next stage in the U.S. moon program was the development of a two-man spacecraft capable of performing moon-related activities. Project Gemini was designed to find out how humans would react to an extended stay in space, to practice rendezvous and docking procedures needed on a moon voyage, and to gain experience with EVA.

NASA scheduled a total of twelve flights for the two-year program. Four of the first five manned flights concentrated on the first objective. Two-man Gemini crews accumulated progressively longer space time: three orbits for *Gemini 3*, four days for *Gemini 4*, eight days for *Gemini 5*, and fourteen days for *Gemini 7*.

Experiments on rendezvous and docking proved to be more difficult. The first failed completely. An Agena target rocket was to be fired into space as a target for docking with *Gemini 6*. But the Agena never reached orbit. NASA

Top: *Alan Shepard during the first U.S. mission in space, May 5, 1961*
Bottom: *the interior of the* Mercury *capsule that Shepard rode in*

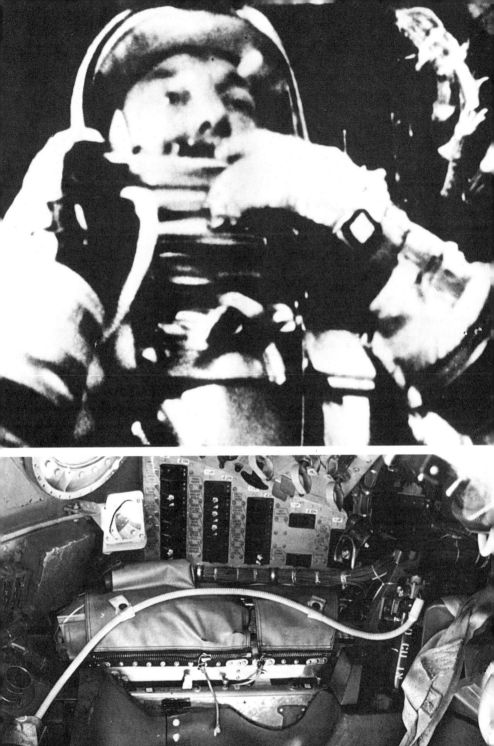

then devised a brilliant (if nerve-racking) last-minute change of plans. *Gemini 6* was removed from the launch platform and was replaced by *Gemini 7*. Then, eleven days after *Gemini 7* was launched, *Gemini 6* was returned to its platform and launched also. Once in orbit, *Gemini 6* used *Gemini 7* (in place of the lost Agena) as its target for docking.

The substitute plan was a success. Astronaut Schirra maneuvered the *Gemini 6* to within 30 cm (12 in) of *Gemini 7* before backing off and returning to earth. By the flights of *Gemini 10, 11,* and *12* (in July, September, and November 1966), rendezvous and docking procedures had become routine.

Experiences with EVA became increasingly more sophisticated with each Gemini flight also. Edward White's twenty-three-minute EVA from *Gemini 4* involved little more than maneuvering in space and photographing the earth. Four EVA experiences later, on *Gemini 12*, astronaut Edwin Aldrin performed nineteen distinct tasks during a two-hour, six-minute EVA. The results were in. The United States was ready for a trip to the moon.

A TIME FOR SECOND THOUGHTS

In its retelling, the Mercury-Gemini story sounds almost too good to be true. A nearly continuous series of triumphs, each step a bit more complex, a bit closer to the first human footprint on the moon. And that synopsis is an accurate tale of progress on the scientific front.

But all was not progressing as smoothly in the political realm. The great rush of enthusiasm for President Kennedy's May 1961 speech had begun to fade. By 1963, the United States had entered a period of détente with the Soviets. Suddenly, a space race with our new almost-friends seemed less crucial to our national survival. For the first time, critics began to question the investment of billions of tax dollars on a moon race that appeared to have few practical benefits for the man or woman in the street.

At first, complaints centered on two aspects of the space program. First, some observers worried about the pace of the Apollo program. They feared that Kennedy's end-of-the-decade challenge was costing too much money and posing too much danger to our astronauts. They often objected not to the space program itself, but to its frantic pace.

Writing in the *Washington Post* on September 24, 1963, for example, columnist Walter Lippman complained that President Kennedy's decision to put a man on the moon had "transformed what is an immensely fascinating scientific experiment into a morbid and vulgar stunt." The same week the *Wall Street Journal* reported that "a majority of a broad cross-section of Americans" interviewed by its reporters were concerned about the pace of the lunar program.[25]

A second issue in the debate was the question of manned versus unmanned flight. Critics pointed out that whatever scientific and political advantages the United States would gain by placing a *human* (rather than a robot) on the moon were hardly worth the additional expense. The Soviets, for example, had claimed that their unmanned explorations of the moon would cost only 5 percent of a comparable manned flight.

These controversies led, in 1963, to the first vigorous debate over NASA's budget since its founding in 1958. Administration officials and NASA administrators were hard-pressed to convince suddenly critical legislators of the value of the "by-the-end-of-the-decade" program. And they were only partially successful. The budget for 1964 rose only modestly over the previous year (from $5.1 billion to $5.25 billion) before beginning to fall back to $5.18 billion in 1966, $4.97 billion in 1967, $4.59 billion in 1968, and $3.4 billion in 1969.

The continued decline in NASA's budget suggests that concerns about the nation's space program did not end in 1963. In fact, the ascension of Lyndon Johnson to the presidency in November 1963 marked yet another turning point in the history of U.S. space efforts. For one thing, Johnson's Great Society programs placed enormous demands on the federal treasury. With limited funds, the president and Congress had to make hard choices: another Apollo flight or two hundred new day-care centers, for example. Thus the space debate became more relevant to ordinary citizens. The issue was no longer "Is a U.S. space program a good thing?" but "Is a U.S. space program more important than housing, education, and health for me and my neighbors?" Whether Johnson's Great Society raised living conditions or not, it certainly raised expectations.

Johnson's ongoing involvement in Vietnam placed yet another strain on the space program. As the United States committed more men and money to the Asian war, the issue was no longer just "rockets versus bread and butter." It was now "rockets versus guns versus bread and butter." In the next chapter, we'll see how these pressures dramatically altered the U.S. space program of the 1970s.

TRAGEDY AND TRIUMPH

NASA officials were very much concerned in 1963 about the public, political, and financial support they needed for the space program. Fortunately, they had one powerful debating point on their side: They were experiencing huge successes in their Mercury and Gemini programs. And they could look forward to the new Project Apollo with considerable confidence.

The "end-of-the-decade" challenge by President Kennedy had seemed bold—perhaps foolhardy and unrealistic—in 1961. At the conclusion of the Gemini program, that goal suddenly seemed within reach. The final stage of the moon program, Project Apollo, would carry two-man teams first in earth orbit, then in lunar orbit, and finally to the surface of the moon itself.

After the stunning successes of the Mercury and Gemini programs, the first event in Project Apollo was a bitter disappointment. During a preflight test of the *Apollo 1* space capsule on January 27, 1967, fire broke out in the command module. The three astronauts inside the capsule, Virgil Grissom, Edward White, and Roger Chafee, all lost their lives.

The *Apollo 1* (whose ground tests were designated as *Apollo 204*) disaster suddenly changed the emphasis of the U.S. space program. For the next eighteen months,

NASA engineers restudied and redesigned the Apollo spacecraft. Then, on October 11, 1968, U.S. manned spaceflight was under way again with the 163-earth-orbit flight of *Apollo 7*. (*Apollo 4, 5,* and *6* were unmanned tests of the Saturn booster rocket.) Once again, everything was "go" for the first moon launch.

That flight, *Apollo 8*, took place between December 21 and 27, 1968. After reaching the moon, astronauts Frank Borman, James Lovell, and William Anders went into lunar orbit. During their twenty-hour, ten-orbit trip around the moon, the space travelers took photographs of the lunar surface and sent live television pictures back to earth.

Apollo 9 and *10* were the final dress rehearsals for a lunar landing. On each of the two flights, the lunar module (LM), which would land on the moon's surface, separated from the command and service module (CSM), which would remain in lunar orbit. The LM was then maneuvered in space and finally redocked with the CSM.

Finally, on July 16, 1969, the crowning achievement of the U.S. space program was at hand. *Apollo 11* lifted off Launchpad 39A at the Kennedy Space Center (KSC) near Cape Canaveral, Florida. On July 20, astronauts Neil Armstrong and Edwin Aldrin stepped onto the moon's surface. The race for the moon was over.

THE END OF THE "SPACE RACE"?

For nearly a decade, the U.S. space program had been predicated on the idea that we were in a "race" to get to the moon before the Soviets. But how true was that assumption? Did the Soviets, in fact, *ever* really hope to place a human on the moon? That point has been in dispute for more than two decades.

On the other hand, we have Soviet statements both prior to and following the success of *Apollo 11* that they had never really had any plans to put a manned spacecraft on the moon. The "race" was strictly a figment of U.S. imagination, they claimed. As early as 1964, Premier Leonid Brezhnev had said that "we Soviet people do not look upon our space exploration as an end in itself, as some

sort of 'race.' The spirit of gamblers is profoundly alien to us in the great and serious business of exploring and conquering outer space."[26]

Some U.S. observers accepted this Soviet position. A 1969 book entitled *Journey to Tranquility* argued that "the struggle to get an American on the Moon by 1970 thrived on an overwhelming fear of Russian space superiority, a fear that NASA still fosters as a challenge to American security and prestige. But by 1963 it had become clear that the Russians had little immediate interest in the Moon and that the race for space did not, in fact, exist."[27]

A great deal of evidence exists, however, that this was not the case. In the first place, many official Soviet statements throughout the decade of the 1960s suggested a concerted Soviet plan to place humans on the moon. For example, cosmonaut Leonov reported in 1969 that "the Soviet Union also is making preparations for a manned flight to the Moon, like the Apollo program of the United States. The Soviet Union will be able to send men to the Moon this year or in 1970."[28]

Also, by the end of the decade, the Soviets were clearly developing the kind of hardware that would be needed for a manned landing on the moon. Between 1968 and 1970, for example, the Soviets launched four unmanned Zond capsules to the moon and back. These appear to have been modified Soyuz spaceships that were, according to U.S. space expert James E. Oberg, "entirely capable of carrying at least one pilot out to the moon and back to earth. . . ."[29]

But once *Apollo 11* had landed on the moon, in contrast to all earlier statements and evidence of the Zond flights, the Soviets simply announced that they had never really been in the race which they had just lost.

Exploring the moon

8
LIVING
IN SPACE

The success of *Apollo 11* was both a remarkable scientific achievement and a real public-relations triumph for the United States. Americans and their supporters worldwide no longer had to settle for "second-best" in their space competition with the Soviets. Yet, in some ways, *Apollo 11* was, as soon as the mission was over, something of a letdown. The focus of the U.S. space program for more than eight years had been on *this* flight. How does one follow an act like that?

To be sure, additional flights in the Apollo program were planned, and each succeeding mission became more sophisticated, returning more data about the moon. By *Apollo 15, 16,* and *17,* U.S. astronauts were using "moon buggies" (*Lunar Rovers*) similar to the Soviets' automated *Lunokhod*s. Only the near disaster of *Apollo 13* spoiled the run of U.S. successes.

On this flight, an oxygen tank on the service module exploded, disabling the spacecraft. Only by ingenious manipulation of their remaining capsule resources and the laws of physics were astronauts John Swigert, James Lovell, and Fred Haise able to return safely to the earth.

But by July 15, 1975, when *Apollo 19* lifted off Pad 39A at KSC, the American public had become fairly blasé about moon travel. No longer was the announcement of a moon landing the cause for millions of Americans to rush to their television sets, there to be captivated by the marvels of modern space science. Indeed, the U.S. Congress had become so disenchanted with the cost of the space program that it canceled the final three flights. *Apollo 19,* part of the joint U.S./USSR Apollo-Soyuz Test Project, was the last launch in the Apollo Lunar Project.

Furthermore, congressional cutbacks had already extended to the second major division of Project Apollo, the Apollo Applications Program (AAP), better known as Skylab. Originally, the AAP was designed to run concurrently with the Apollo Lunar Project. Its aims were to investigate in more detail the effect of extended space travel on humans, to carry out advanced astronomical studies, and to study certain industrial processes carried out under conditions of weightlessness. (These are essentially the same objectives as those of the Soviet Salyut program.)

But by the mid-1970s, Congress had withdrawn financing for the greatest portion of AAP. All that remained of the original two-workshop, seven-crew program was a single Skylab station to be visited by three crews of astronauts.

SKYLAB
The Skylab program consisted of two phases. First, the unoccupied orbital workshop itself was to be launched and placed into earth orbit. Then, three separate crews of three astronauts each were to rendezvous and dock with the workshop. The three crews would eventually stay and work in Skylab for twenty-eight days, fifty-nine days, and eighty-four days.

The first two minutes of the nine months of the Skylab program were by far the most difficult. Only sixty-three seconds after lift-off, the meteoroid shield on the workshop ripped off. The shield was designed both to protect the workshop from meteoroids and to shield the capsule from intense solar radiation. When the shield broke loose, it also tore off one of the solar cell wings and trapped the other wing in its folded position. Thus, although the workshop reached orbit according to schedule, it had lost a vital temperature control system and its main source of electric power.

Skylab 2, carrying the first three astronauts to the station, was scheduled for launch on May 15, 1973. That launch was delayed by ten days, however, as NASA engineers frantically attempted to solve the temperature and power problems. The method they finally devised required the *Skylab 2* crew to conduct an extended EVA from the workshop. On the EVA, the astronauts were to (1) erect an umbrellalike structure above the Skylab to shield it from the sun, and (2) cut loose the damaged meteoroid shield and free the solar cell wings.

One day after docking with *Skylab,* Astronauts Charles Conrad, Paul Weitz, and Joseph Kerwin performed two EVAs during which they remedied the station's problems. Temperatures inside the workshop dropped rapidly from 54°C (130°F) to 38°C (100°F) and finally to a constant 24°C (75°F). And electric power began flowing from the solar cell wings as soon as they were freed during the EVA.

Skylab 4 *(U.S.)*

Except for a few minor problems, the remaining portion of the three Skylab flights was rather uneventful. During their stays on the space station, the nine astronauts conducted extensive medical observations and experiments on themselves, made visual and photographic studies of earth resources, carried out continuous studies of the sun, observed comet Kohoutek, completed a number of industrial and processing experiments, and performed dozens of other miscellaneous experiments. The *Skylab 4* crew returned to earth on February 8, 1974. The United States would not put a human into space again for just over seven years.

THE EARLY SOYUZ PROGRAM

The U.S. Skylab project in 1973 was a brief "fling" at a manned earth-orbital space program. The Soviet Union had inaugurated a smiliar program—using Salyut space stations—two years earlier and have maintained that program on a continuous basis ever since.

Earlier we saw how Sergei Korolev had planned to develop a larger, more sophisticated space capsule following the completion of the Vostok/Voskhod program. The new capsule produced by the Soyuz program was ready for launch in April 1967, only four months after the *Apollo 204* tragedy. Ironically, the Soviets were also to experience a terrible disaster on the first test of their new spacecraft.

The launch of *Soyuz 1* on April 23 appeared to go smoothly. Western observers were a bit puzzled when the flight ended after only eighteen orbits (one day), however. A solo flight of this duration represented little or no progress beyond the Vostok flights. Still, there seemed to be no problem with the capsule's reentry . . . until the last moments of the flight. Then the parachute system which was to carry the capsule to the ground failed to deploy properly. With nothing to slow its speed, *Soyuz 1* crashed to earth, killing its pilot cosmonaut Vladimir Komarov.

The *Soyuz 1* disaster had much the same effect on Soviet space science as did the *Apollo 204* tragedy on its U.S. counterpart. The Soviets canceled all scheduled flights and devoted the next eighteen months to the redesign of the Soyuz spacecraft and to testing unmanned versions of the capsule (all given Kosmos designations).

On October 25 and 26, 1968, the Soviets renewed the Soyuz program with two launches, the unmanned *Soyuz 2,* and *Soyuz 3,* carrying Col. Georgi Beregovoy. Beregovoy conducted a successful rendezvous with *Soyuz 2,* but was unable to dock with his target. (Some authorities believe that *Soyuz 2* and *3* were not even equipped for docking.) That feat was accomplished three months later, however, when docking occurred between *Soyuz 4* (carrying one cosmonaut) and *Soyuz 5* (carrying three cosmonauts). During docking, two of the *Soyuz 5* cosmonauts left their ship and transferred to *Soyuz 4,* in which they returned to earth.

Whether the Soyuz flights were ever meant to be preliminaries in a possible manned flight (like the comparable Gemini flights) is something we will probably never know for sure. In any case, by the time of the next Soyuz flights, that objective had almost certainly been dismissed. *Soyuz 6, 7,* and *8* were launched, respectively, on October 11, 12, and 13, 1969, three months after *Apollo 11* had reached the moon. To both the Soviets and the rest of the world, the goal of the Soyuz program was now clear: to conduct many kinds of research aboard earth-orbiting spacecraft.

A major success in the early stages of that program was *Soyuz 9,* launched on June 1, 1970. The spacecraft, carrying Andrian Nikolayev and Vitaliy Serastyanov, had no rendezvous or docking capabilities; the flight was designed primarily to test the effects of extended periods in space on the spacecraft and its crew. During their eighteen days in space, the crew conducted medical measurements on themselves, such as pulse and respiration rates, before and after exercise; sensitivity to pain; energy expenditure; and hand strength. They also carried out biological experiments on cells, bacteria, insects, and flowering plants. Finally, they completed physical experiments and measurements on terrestrial features, their own orbital characteristics, and various celestial bodies.

THE SPACE STATION ERA

Since 1971, the Soviet manned spaceflight program has developed along the lines of the U.S. Skylab project (although, of course, it predated the U.S. program by at least two years). In the Soviet pattern, an unmanned workshop designated as a Salyut space station is placed into orbit. Then other manned and/or unmanned spacecraft are also launched for rendezvous and docking with the *Salyut.*

The first workshop, *Salyut 1,* was launched on April 19, 1971. Three days later, *Soyuz 10,* carrying three cosmonauts, also went into orbit. The *Soyuz* successfully docked with *Salyut 1,* but the crew did not board the unmanned space station. Soviet news accounts claimed that the mission was a complete success, but Western observers suspect that a technical malfunction may have prevented the expected crew transfer and a longer stay in orbit. In any case, *Soyuz 10* returned to earth after only thirty-two orbits (two days).

The second flight to *Salyut 1, Soyuz 11,* lifted off on June 6, 1971. This time the three cosmonauts were able to rendezvous, dock, and board the space station. They spent the next twenty-three days in orbit, checking out the station's equipment and systems, carrying out earth resource studies, performing atmospheric research, and conducting biological and medical experiments on themselves.

The return of *Soyuz 11* to earth appeared routine. But when the recovery team opened the landed capsule, they found all three cosmonauts dead. The Soviets did not comment on the cause of the disaster until nearly two years later. Then they explained that a pressure valve in the capsule had not closed properly during descent. Air leaked out of the cabin, and all three cosmonauts suffocated. (Since the flight of *Voskhod 1,* Soviet cosmonauts on all flights except *Soyuz 4, 5,* and *6* had worn no pressure suits during their flight. They resumed doing so as of *Soyuz 12.*)

As with earlier U.S. and Soviet space disasters, the *Soyuz 11* tragedy changed the course of Soviet space research for a long time. For nearly two years, Soviet engineers worked on a redesigned Soyuz spacecraft.

During this time, a number of Kosmos flights were apparently tests of the rebuilt capsule. Then, on September 27, 1973, manned spaceflight resumed with the launch and two-day flight of *Soyuz 12.*

Meanwhile, an attempt to launch a second orbital workshop, *Salyut 2,* apparently had failed earlier in April of the same year. After having spent eleven days in orbit, the workshop apparently developed some serious malfunction and was destroyed. Western observers believe that *Salyut 2* (and all succeeding even-numbered space stations) was a military project.

The next attempt to launch a Salyut station, on June 25, 1974, was successful. This station stayed in orbit until January 24, 1975, when it reentered the earth's atmosphere over the Pacific Ocean. During its time in space, *Salyut 3* was visited successfully for fourteen days by *Soyuz 14* and unsuccessfully by *Soyuz 15.* (It was unable to dock.)

SUCCESS FOR THE SALYUT SPACE STATIONS

Since 1974, four more Salyut workshops have been launched into orbit. Each station has become more sophisticated, and the uses to which they have been put, more advanced and elaborate. *Salyut 4* (December 26, 1974, to February 2, 1977) was visited by cosmonauts from *Soyuz 17* (for thirty days) and Soyuz *18* (for sixty-three days). The length of the second stay showed that the Soviets had found ways to reduce any physical deterioration that humans might experience in space.

Salyut 5 (June 22, 1976, to August 8, 1977) was the least successful of recent orbiting laboratories. The three-man crew from *Soyuz 21* stayed forty-nine days but returned earlier than planned. And *Soyuz 23* failed to dock with the station and returned only two days after lift-off.

Top: *artist's conception of a* Salyut-Soyuz *linkup*
Bottom: *on board* Salyut 7

Although the first months of *Salyut 6* (September 29, 1977, to July 29, 1982) were not very promising, this station eventually marked a turning point in the Soviet manned space program. Two weeks after *Salyut 6* reached orbit, a two-man *Soyuz 25* team was unable to dock with the station. At first, Soviet engineers feared that the problem was with the Salyut docking port. Had this been the case, the greatly expanded and improved new *Salyut* might well have been a total loss.

Soviet officials decided on a bold effort to find out why the *Soyuz 25* docking had failed. *Soyuz 26* was launched into orbit and managed to dock at the second docking port of *Salyut 6*. (This was the first time the Soviets had reported that *Salyut 6* had docking ports at both ends of the station.)

Then cosmonaut Georgiy Grechko carried out an eighty-eight minute EVA (the first Soviet EVA in nearly nine years) to examine the opposite docking port. He found absolutely no problem with the port, indicating that future docks should be able to proceed without difficulty. (No explanation has ever been offered for the failed docking of *Soyuz 25*.)

After this time, the *Salyut 6* record was one of almost uninterrupted records and successes. The *Soyuz 26* crew stayed on board the station for a record ninety-six days. One month after their arrival at the station, the *Soyuz 26* crew was joined by another pair of cosmonauts in *Soyuz 27,* which docked successfully at the previously troublesome port. The two crews spent five days together on the station. Then the *Soyuz 27* crew returned to earth in the *Soyuz 26* spacecraft, leaving its own ship docked to the *Salyut.* The Soviets were eager to test this ship-exchange technique since spacecraft tend to deteriorate after a certain time in orbit. This method, however, allows a crew to spend a virtually unlimited amount of time on the station.

Less than a week later, yet another space first was recorded. A new kind of spacecraft, *Progress 1,* was launched, reached orbit, and docked at the empty *Salyut 6* port. The *Progress* was an unmanned space "freighter" or space "tug" designed to resupply the space station.

The first of these new tugs delivered fuel, new life-support materials, and an electric furnace to the cosmonauts between January 22 and February 6, 1978. A third cosmonaut crew also visited *Salyut 6* from March 2 to 10.

During its remaining time in orbit, *Salyut 6* was visited by twelve more manned Soyuz spacecrafts, one unmanned Soyuz supply ship, and eleven Progress space tugs. One flight *(Soyuz 33)* failed to dock. Finally, one test vehicle of the new, upgraded Soyuz T series, *Soyuz T-1,* docked successfully on December 15, 1975. The Soviets also announced that *Soyuz 40,* which visited *Salyut 6* on May 14, 1981, was the last of the older Soyuz model capsules to be launched.

The most recent Salyut space station, *Salyut 7,* was placed into orbit on April 19, 1982. The Soviets have used *Salyut 7* much as they did *Salyut 6,* supplying it by means of Progress tugs and Soyuz-T flights.

In 1984 a crew from *Soyuz T-10* visited and occupied *Salyut 7* for a record two hundred thirty-seven days. During their stay, two of the three-man crew made a total of six space walks for the purpose of repairing a leak in a fuel line and attaching a new set of solar panels.

Two other Soyuz T crews also made brief visits to the space station while the *Soyuz T-10* crew was in residence. *Soyuz T-11* carried the first Indian cosmonaut, while the *Soyuz T-12* crew included Svetlana Savistskaya, the first woman to fly in space twice and the first woman to complete a space walk.

All told, the six Soviet EVAs took twenty-two hours, fifty minutes, slightly more than the previous *Skylab 4* record of twenty-two hours, twenty-five minutes.

Salyut 7 has experienced some difficulties, however. In January 1985, radio communications between the station and ground control at Star City were lost. Within a short time, the station had lost its "fix" on the sun, and its water system froze. Soon its electrical instruments stopped functioning and also froze. The station began to tumble out of control, and Soviet officials announced that "in view of the fact that the planned program of work on the Salyut 7 station has been fulfilled completely, at the

present time the station has been deactivated and is con-
tinuing its flight in automatic mode."[30] Most observers felt
that this was the death announcement for the station.
However, a remarkable rescue mission by the *Soyuz
T-13* crew turned this potential disaster into a great triumph.
The crew, consisting of Vladimir Dzhanibekov and Viktor
Savinyhk, was able to dock with *Salyut 7* on June 8, 1985.
The next day they entered the station to find conditions
even worse than ground control had expected.

With great skill and patience, the cosmonauts were able
to reorient the station's solar panels and recharge its on-
board batteries. Within a few days, the station's internal
temperature began to rise, its water system thawed, and
most instruments began to operate normally. By the end
of June, a Progress tug had delivered supplies to the
station and it was in nearly normal working condition again.

In February 1986 the Soviets launched *Mir*, a new space
station. Two cosmonauts flew to *Mir* in a *Soyuz* spacecraft
and spent over four months aboard the space station
before returning to earth.

THE U.S. SPACE
TRANSPORTATION (SHUTTLE) SYSTEM

In the long run, any program for an earth-orbiting space
station must consist of two parts. The first is the station
itself, a module in which people can live and work for long
periods of time. Skylab and Salyut are examples of such
stations. Thus far, the Soviet Union has devoted far more
time and energy to this aspect of a manned station than
has the United States.

The second requirement for an earth-orbiting station is
a dependable and economical way of getting to and from
the workstation. Thus far, the Soviets have devoted relatively little attention to this part of the problem. As of
early 1987, they are still using disposable rockets to get
cosmonauts, fuel, and supplies to their *Salyut*s. Although
this system works well enough, it is much too expensive
on a long-term basis.

U.S. space scientists, on the other hand, have chosen
to work on the transportation part of the space station
system and have done little (beyond Skylab) on the station

itself. The official name for the U.S. system is the Space Transportation System (STS), although it is much better known as the space shuttle.

Ideas for an STS go back to the writings of early space pioneers like Tsiolkovsky, Goddard, and the German rocket specialist, Hermann Oberth. By 1954, U.S. rocket scientists like Wernher von Braun were even describing such a system in the popular magazine *Colliers*. After more than five years of preliminary studies by NASA, President Richard Nixon approved the construction of a space shuttle on January 5, 1972.

The space shuttle system consists of two components: the propulsion system and the orbiter. The propulsion system provides the enormous power needed to get the orbiter into space. It includes two solid-rocket boosters (SRBs) and an external tank (ET) containing liquid oxygen and liquid hydrogen. After the SRBs and ET have accomplished their task of lifting the orbiter into space, they fall back to earth. The SRBs are recovered and used again, while the ET burns up as it reenters the earth's atmosphere.

The orbiter is about the size of a DC-9 jet airliner. The two-level cabin in its forward section includes living, working, and storage space for the shuttle crew. The crew consists of the mission commander, pilot, mission specialists, payload specialists, and passengers. Mission specialists are regular astronauts familiar with the shuttle itself as well as with all experiments and payloads carried by the shuttle. Payload specialists are noncareer astronauts who have expert knowledge about a particular experiment or payload. And passengers are one-time travelers on the shuttle, along to experience spaceflight first hand.

One of the major goals of shuttle flight is to carry on experiments that cannot be done, or cannot be done as efficiently, on earth. For example, the first payload specialist was Dr. Charles Walker of the McDonnell Douglas Corporation. Dr. Walker's speciality is continuous flow electrophoresis, a method for producing very pure pharmaceuticals in space.

The largest space in the orbiter is occupied by the cargo

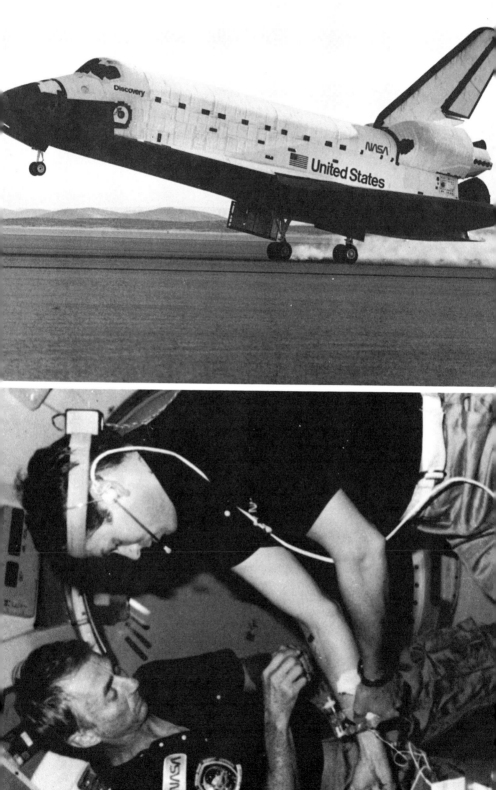

bay, where large objects such as satellites and the Space-lab are carried into space.

Between February and October 1977, thirteen initial flights were conducted on an experimental shuttle, *Orbiter 101*, the *Enterprise*. A major problem detected during these trial flights involved the orbiter's thirty-six thousand heat shield tiles. Designed to protect the orbiter during reentry, many of the tiles came loose during launch and landing in the test flights. Not until four years later was this problem adequately resolved. Then, on April 12, 1981, John W. Young and Robert L. Crippen rode Space Shuttle *Orbiter 102* (*Columbia*) on a two-day, six-hour orbital flight before landing safely at Edwards Air Force Base in California.

Columbia soon began to fly on a regular basis about three times a year. It was joined by *Orbiter 103* (*Challenger*) in April 1983; *Orbiter 104* (*Discovery*) in June 1984; and *Orbiter 105* (*Atlantis*) in April 1985.

The shuttle program has experienced some extraordinary sucessess and failures in its brief history. By the end of 1983, the shuttle was being used on a routine basis to carry out experiments in space and to deliver new satellites to orbit. *STS-9* also carried *Spacelab* into orbit on November 28, 1983.

By 1984, the shuttle was regularly carrying out another of its major missions: the capture and repair of damaged or malfunctioning satellites. In April of that year, the crew of *STS 41-C* was able to retrieve the Solar Maximum Mission ("Solar Max") satellite, which had been launched in 1980. The satellite had malfunctioned shortly after reaching orbit and had been essentially useless ever since. Members of the *STS 41-C* crew successfully captured the satellite, returned it to the shuttle cargo bay, made necessary repairs, and returned it to orbit.

Top: *the space shuttle* Discovery
Bottom: *drawing blood during a shuttle mission*

As part of the retrieval process, astronaut George Nelson flew through space in a "Manned Maneuvering Unit" (MMU). The MMU allows an astronaut to work in space without a tether line holding him or her to the shuttle. The MMU had first been tested successfully on the preceding shuttle flight by astronaut Bruce McCandless. Later in the same year, the crew of *STS 51-A* carried out an equally spectacular operation. They successfully captured two malfunctioning satellites, Indonesia's *Palapa-B2* and Western Union's *WESTAR 6*, returned them to the shuttle's cargo bay, and brought them back to earth for repairs.

The seemingly endless record of shuttle successes came to a sudden and horrible end on January 28, 1986, when *Orbiter 103*, *Challenger*, exploded only seventy-three seconds after lift-off from Pad 39A. All seven astronauts aboard the flight lost their lives.

WHERE NEXT FOR THE U.S.?

President Ronald Reagan appointed former Secretary of State William Rogers to head a committee to investigate the *Challenger* disaster. The committee found that the explosion was caused by a faulty O-ring gasket that allowed hot gases to escape from one of the shuttle's solid boosters.

The committee did not end its investigation with this technical finding, however. It also analyzed the administrative process by which decisions were being made in the STS program. They learned that mechanical problems were not unusual with shuttle equipment. In fact, engineers had warned about possible failure of the gaskets more than two years before the *Challenger* disaster.

Perhaps the most significant finding the committee came to was that NASA officials had simply pushed the shuttle program too hard and too fast. They had felt obligated to present the STS program as a dependable, operational space transportation system that could function efficiently when, in fact, that simply wasn't the case. The goal of twenty-four shuttle flights each year by 1988 turned out to have been overly optimistic.

The U.S. space program suffered two further setbacks in the months following the *Challenger* explosion when two "old reliable" rockets, a NASA Delta and an air force Titan 34D, both exploded during lift-off.

By mid-1986, then, legislators, administration officials, space scientists, and average citizens were beginning to wonder what the fate of the U.S. space program was to be, given these failures of equipment. In particular, President Reagan was confronted with some difficult and fundamental questions about the nation's space policy.

First, he had to decide whether or not to replace the lost *Challenger* spacecraft. Second, he had to rethink the objectives and operation of the STS. Third, he had to decide what direction the U.S. space program was to take in the coming years. By the end of 1986, some of those decisions were being made.

First, the president authorized the replacement of *Challenger* with a new shuttle at an estimated cost of $2.7 billion. NASA then announced that the next shuttle flight would be conducted on February 18, 1988. Second, the president decided to alter the way in which shuttles were to be used. He directed that no further contracts with private organizations be signed and that all further shuttle missions be restricted to government missions. Private industries learned that they would have to build their own rockets and delivery systems or find other governments and agencies to launch satellites for them.

By 1987, private industries had begun to do just that. In January 1987, for example, Teresat, Inc., of New York, signed a contract with the Chinese government to launch its WESTAR-6S communication satellite.

Some critics have been suggesting that the United States has not had a coherent space program since the Apollo project or, perhaps, the STS program. They argue that our space activities are fragmented and somewhat haphazard. The *Challenger* disaster, they believe, only highlighted our previous failure to define our future space objectives and to develop a clear program to meet those objectives.

One science writer has gone so far as to suggest that NASA may never fully recover from the damage done to its presitge and reliability by the *Challenger* loss.[31]

NASA is presently developing plans for cooperative

space activities with the Soviet Union, for manned flights to Mars, and for the construction of an orbiting space station. Yet the nation's highest advisory committees on space sciences are still not satisfied that we really know where we're going in space over the next decade. In a report published in August 1986, for example, NASA's Space Advisory Council expressed the view that "actions being taken by the U.S. to restore its space launch capability are neither adequate nor sufficiently rapid," and, more generally, that "the Nation has allowed its space technology base to erode, leaving it with little technological capability to move out in new directions should the need arise. . . . [Unless actions are taken very soon] the U.S. civil space program will continue to erode, to the Nation's great detriment."[32]

It seems likely that the late 1980s and early 1990s will be a period of important reassessment as to what space research means, if anything, to Americans. It may well be a challenge for the nation unlike anything since the days of *Sputnik 1*.

9 | THE PRESENT AND THE FUTURE

Events that occur in space are *international* events. The United States or USSR cannot launch a satellite that will travel over its own country only. In fact, one of the main reasons that many satellites are put into orbit is that they *do* travel high above other countries.

A major objective of the early U.S. satellite program, for example, was to orbit a satellite that could collect information about Soviet military capabilities. Until 1960, U.S. intelligence had relied on very high flying U-2 reconnaissance planes for this information. But when the Soviets shot down one of these planes in 1960, American military planners had no other reliable replacement. Suddenly "spy satellites" became an important part of our nation's intelligence-gathering operation.

WHO OWNS SPACE?
The use of spy satellites (or any other kind of satellite) raises some difficult political and legal questions, however. The fundamental issue is: Who owns space? We can say, for example, the Soviet Union has legitimate legal authority over the city of Kiev, or any other land or water mass within Soviet borders. And, over the years, nations have acknowledged that the air space above a

nation belongs to that nation. That "air space" has come to be defined as the height to which an airplane can fly.

But when *Sputnik 1* was launched, this legal issue took on new meaning. In terms of air space, how far up did a nation's authority extend: to 7 km (4 mi), 20 km (12 mi), 100 km (60 mi), to the moon? This question was certainly a practical one because everyone had agreed that the U-2 destroyed by the Soviets had violated its air space. Would a spy satellite passing over Soviet soil eighteen times a day do so also?

At first, the United States and USSR dodged this question in imaginative ways. The Soviets said, for example, that *Sputnik 1* violated no international laws since it was simply traveling in space while the countries of the world passed beneath it! And the United States simply launched its spy satellites and ignored any objections to their legal status.

DEFINING SPACE LAW

Most nations of the world realized, however, that at least some statement on space law was needed. In November 1958, the United Nations (UN) established an Ad Hoc Committee on the Peaceful Uses of Outer Space (COPUOS), an organization through which members of the UN would eventually develop a policy on international space law.

COPUOS did not reach consensus easily. Both the Soviet Union and the United States had a great deal at stake in the policy the Committee would finally adopt. Little wonder, then, that more than five years would pass before COPUOS was able to write a document to which the full UN could agree. That statement, A Declaration of Legal Principles Governing Activities of States in the Exploration and Use of Outer Space, passed the UN General Assembly on December 13, 1963.

The Declaration confirmed some lofty notions about space: that outer space "belonged" to no one nation, but was open and free to exploration by all; that space activities should be carried out for purposes that would benefit all humans; and that nations were legally responsible for their own spacecraft and any harm that might be done by them.

The Declaration, like the UN Charter itself, is an admirable statement of principles. It clearly defines outer space as an area open to research and use by all nations. However, it ignores some important, but still controversial, questions about the use of outer space, such as the role of military spacecraft. One can imagine that with increased activity in space by more nations the 1963 Declaration will eventually need to be revised and updated.

JOINT ACTIVITIES IN SPACE

For many years, references to "international" issues in space were misleading. In fact, only two nations had the capability of conducting space research: the United States and USSR. However, both space powers have long recognized the political (and, sometimes, technological) advantages of inviting other nations to participate with them. The U.S. interest in international cooperation was stated in the founding document of NASA, which called for "the promotion of cooperation with other nations in space science and technology."

The first concrete evidence of that intent was the launch in 1962 of an earth satellite, *Ariel 1*, which carried a payload contributed by the United Kingdom. In succeeding years, other joint projects have involved Canada, Italy, France, West Germany, the Netherlands, Spain, Japan, Indonesia, and the European Space Agency (ESA). Intelsat has also involved U.S. space communication projects with more than a hundred other nations. In joint projects such as these, each participating nation is responsible for some specific task: designing an experiment or building a piece of equipment, for example.

The Soviet Union came somewhat later to international projects and has pursued them, in many cases, for more blatantly propagandistic purposes. As a part of its Kosmos program, the Soviets initiated a series of *Interkosmos* launchings in 1968. Flights in this series, like those of the U.S. program, have carried payloads from nations such as Bulgaria, Czechoslovakia, East Germany, Hungary,

Poland, Romania, France, and India. Their Intersputnik program is, like Intelsat, also an international venture.

Perhaps the most dramatic Soviet display of internationalism, however, has been the joint Soyuz flights that began in 1978. On these flights, one or two Soviet cosmonauts have been joined by a "guest cosmonaut" from another nation. For the initial flight in this series, *Soyuz 28*, the Soviets invited a representative of Czechoslovakia to join the trip to *Salyut 6*. Since then, guest cosmonauts have also come from Poland, East Germany, Hungary, Vietnam, Cuba, Mongolia, Romania, and France.

The representative from Bulgaria had an unexpectedly exciting trip when the Soyuz capsule in which he was riding developed problems and was unable to dock with *Salyut 6*. His was the only unsuccessful guest cosmonaut flight.

The guest Soyuz flights appear to have had little purpose other than to demonstrate Soviet solidarity with its allies. According to one authority, the primary criteria in selecting guest cosmonauts have been "ease of training and political reliability." In most cases, the guest cosmonauts are "not allowed to interfere with the work of the permanent crewmen" and are regarded as something of an annoyance by the Soyuz regulars. The major exception to that rule appears to have been the active collaboration of the French cosmonaut Jean-Loup Chrétien in the June 1982 flight of *Soyuz T-6*.

Western observers were not even able to understand how the Soviets had decided on the sequence in which guest cosmonauts would fly . . . until someone pointed out that the guest cosmonauts in 1978 and 1979 had appeared in alphabetical order according to the Russian alphabet![33]

In recent years, nations other than the United States and the Soviet Union have also developed the ability to launch space vehicles. France launched its first spacecraft in 1965, followed by Australia in 1967, China and Japan in 1970, the United Kingdom in 1971, the European Space Agency in 1979, and India in 1980.

THE APOLLO-SOYUZ TEST PROJECT

In some respects, the most significant international space event to date has been the Apollo-Soyuz Test Project (ASTP). The idea for a joint docking between a U.S. Apollo spacecraft and a Soviet Soyuz capsule developed in the early 1970s. By that time, the "moon race" was long past and a period of détente between the world's two super-powers had begun.

On May 24, 1972, the Soviet Union and the United States signed an agreement to cooperate in the exploration and peaceful uses of outer space, a pact that included plans for the ASTP. Some observers saw the possibility of a "handshake in space" between cosmonauts and astronauts as a symbol of the most promising benefits that might result from space research. Critics argued, however, that ASTP was little more than the latest Soviet scheme for learning U.S. space secrets.

In any case, the ASTP reached fruition in July 1975. On July 15, Soviet cosmonauts Aleksei Leonov and Valeri Kubasov lifted off in their *Soyuz 19* capsule and went into orbit. Seven hours later, the last U.S. Apollo spacecraft to fly lifted off from KSC. After adjusting its orbit to that of *Soyuz 19*, the Apollo spacecraft rendezvoused and docked with its Soviet target on July 17.

During the next two days, the crews exchanged hand-shakes and gifts and conducted eleven experiments, six by the Soviets and five by the two crews together. *Soyuz 19* returned to earth on July 21, and the Apollo spacecraft on July 24, ending a brief but dramatic international effort between the world's two space powers.

THE MILITARY USES OF OUTER SPACE

The final section of this book deals with the uses of space for military purposes. And that's a bit strange. For one thing, the most active debates about space today concern military issues: research on antisatellite weapons and President Reagan's plan for a Strategic Defense Initiative (SDI), for example.

More relevant, however, is the fact that the military has *always* been closely associated with space research in both the United States and the USSR. As one authority has pointed out, during the first decade of the Space Age, "First, and foremost, space was about spying."[34] Another expert has estimated that approximately two-thirds of the three thousand payloads launched by the Soviet Union and the United States since the early 1960s have had military objectives.[35]

Why, then, does the militarization of space receive so little attention in this book? The primary reason is that neither the Soviets nor the United States has much to say about their military programs in space. In fact, the Soviets claim to this day that their space program has *only* peaceful objectives. Military research and applications simply do not exist, they claim.

The United States is only somewhat more open about its military objectives in space. It was sixteen years after the launch of the first U.S. spy satellite, for example, before this government acknowledged that it even had a space reconnaissance program. An official staff report by the Congressional Research Service points out that "it became United States policy from March 1962 on to have no public names for its military space flights, aside from some later exceptions where a variety of other agencies were sharing in the scientific and technological experiments. . . ."[36] A further problem in learning about the military uses of space is the possibility that a single satellite can be used for more than one purpose. Thus, a Transit navigation satellite can monitor the movements of both civilian and military air and sea transportation.

Astronaut Tom Stafford and cosmonaut Alexei Leonov at the interface between an Apollo *spacecraft and* Soyuz 19 *in July 1975*

WEAPONS IN SPACE

All of this is not to say that we have no information at all about the use of space by U.S. and Soviet military forces. On the contrary, nonmilitary space observers have ferreted out a good deal of information on this subject. For example, authorities can set our minds at ease about the one military use of space that probably comes to one's mind first: The orbiting of nuclear weapons. We know that neither the United States nor the USSR has any significant program for placing nuclear weapons into outer space.

The Soviets did conduct extensive research on such a program in the 1960s. Their Fractional Orbit Bombardment Satellites (FOBS) system consisted of satellites carrying bombs, launched into low earth orbit. The FOBS system had the advantage of delivering weapons during the initial orbit (like ICBMs) or calling them down during some later orbital pass.

The United States has not pursued a weapons-in-space program of this kind. The dangers and expense appear too great to make this option viable. The Soviets seem to have agreed with that assessment, since they discontinued work on FOBS in 1971.

MILITARY APPLICATIONS
OF SPACE RESEARCH

Both U.S. and Soviet military scientists have found many other ways to use space, however. For example, probably the great majority of Kosmos satellites have some military mission. In a typical Kosmos flight, the satellite uses high-resolution cameras to take photographs of foreign land areas during its two weeks or so in orbit. At the conclusion of its flight, the satellite returns to earth, carrying with it the photographs taken while in space.

Satellite photographs like these provide extensive information about topics such as the location and nature of U.S. missile launch sites, construction of new military facilities, possible nuclear tests, and the progress of local wars (such as the Iraqi-Iranian war).

The United States has spy satellites similar to those in the Kosmos series. Discover, SAMOS, and MIDAS satellites are all U.S. reconnaissance systems about which the military has occasionally released some (but usually very little) information.

Experts believe that a major emphasis of both the U.S. and USSR manned spaceflight programs has also been military in nature. Prior to the 1986 *Challenger* disaster, for example, 37 percent of all U.S. shuttle flights planned up to 1994 had military missions. One consequence of the *Challenger* accident was President Reagan's decision to remove all civilian commercial missions from future shuttle flights, greatly increasing the military component of that project.

The early stages of that transformation occurred in December 1984. In that month, the Department of Defense created a storm of controversy announcing that the January 1985 launch of its first all-military shuttle flight would be closed to press coverage. (Rumor had it that one purpose of that flight was the release of a new military spy satellite.)

Soviet Salyut space stations appear to have essentially the same military functions as those of the U.S. shuttles. Most authorities believe that at least half the work done by cosmonauts aboard the *Salyut*s is for military purposes.

ANTISATELLITE DEVICES

Perhaps the single most active area of military research in space in recent years involves the development of anti-satellite (ASAT) devices. ASAT weapons are launched into space with the intention of finding and destroying another nation's satellites. In the early 1960s, the United States had an operational ASAT system which made use of nuclear-tipped Thor missiles based on Johnston Island in the Pacific Ocean. That system was dismantled in 1975.

The Soviets have been testing a similar system since 1968. A Soviet ASAT test consists of two launches. The first launch carries a dummy target satellite into orbit. The second launch sends an interceptor satellite in pursuit of the target satellite. The aim is for the interceptor to catch up with, lock onto, and destroy the target during the interceptor's first or second orbit. In the first fourteen years of testing, the Soviets achieved success in only nine of its twenty ASAT launches.

Meanwhile, the United States had renewed its ASAT testing program in 1977. The present U.S. system consists of a Miniature Homing Vehicle (MHV) launched from an F-15 airplane. The MHV is able to locate, track, and attack a satellite in orbit, or even while on its way to orbit. U.S. testing of its MHV system has continued to date in spite of a Soviet moratorium on its ASAT tests. The MHV system became operational in 1987.

THE STRATEGIC
DEFENSE INITIATIVE (SDI)

By the mid-1980s, questions of the military use of space had become a topic of major concern to most American men and women in the street. The cause for this interest was a proposal made by President Ronald Reagan on March 23, 1983. Concerned about what he viewed as a continuing buildup of Soviet missile capability, President Reagan suggested a countereffort by the United States that would make use of the latest in defensive weapons technology.

President Reagan's proposal for a Strategic Defense Initiative called for both land- and space-based weapons. But because of the latter component, the proposal quickly received the nickname "Star Wars."

The fundamental concept behind SDI is the development of a defensive system that will be able to detect the launch of missiles from the Soviet Union or its submarines, seek out those missiles while they are en route to the United States, and destroy them at altitudes high enough to prevent damage to the U.S. population.

Few political or scientific proposals have generated as much debate as has SDI. On the one hand, supporters argue that SDI is the next logical step in the United States'

Star Wars scenario

effort to maintain peace in the world. We must have a way, they insist, to protect ourselves against a missile system which the Soviets are expanding and improving each year. By completing SDI, they believe, the United States will be taking the most meaningful possible step in preventing the use of nuclear weapons by either nation.

Opponents cite a number of objections to SDI. They say that the research needed to put the system into place could cost more than one trillion dollars. With this much money involved, they fear that SDI and the Department of Defense could become the single most powerful force in determining the kind of research and development that takes place in the United States. At that point, we might have realized President Eisenhower's concerns of thirty years earlier when the technological demands of space research overwhelm the democratic system by which R&D are carried out in this country.

Some observers also worry that SDI may violate existing treaties with the Soviets which have worked well, if not perfectly, for many years. Besides, they point out that weapons developed for a *defensive* system can also be used *offensively*. Thus, research on SDI will heat up, not cool down, the arms race. As soon as the Soviets see that the United States is serious about SDI, they will almost certainly feel compelled to increase their own offensive capacity or to develop a "Star Wars" system of their own.

Finally, many scientists oppose SDI because they think the system simply won't work. The technology is so complex, they say, that the system would probably never be more than 50 or 60 percent effective. But even if it was 90, 95, or 98 percent effective, a Soviet missile attack could still result in tens of millions of American casualties.

Supporters of SDI disagree about the possible effectiveness of the program. But even with something less than 100 percent effectiveness, they say, we need to consider the millions of lives that a defensive system like this *would* save. Finally, President Reagan and his adherents see SDI as a crucial bargaining chip in our ongoing weapons negotiations with the Soviet government.

Debates about the military uses of space, in general, and about SDI, in particular, are likely to continue for many years. These debates emphasize the role of space in today's society. The importance of national prestige in space accomplishments is as great today as it was in the days of *Sputnik 1* and *Apollo 11*. The contributions of scientific satellites are as great today as they were during the flights of the *OSO*s, the *Venera*s, and the *Surveyor*s. And the practical values gained from application satellites are as significant today as they were with the launches of the *Molniya*s, the *Meteor*s, and the Intelsat satellites. But in some ways, it may be the decisions that humans make about the military uses of outer space that will determine most profoundly the ultimate course of Soviet and U.S. societies.

NOTES

1. William Shelton, *Soviet Space Exploration: The First Decade* (New York: Washington Square Press, 1968), 5.
2. U.S. Congress, Senate, *Soviet Space Programs, 1962–65*, Staff Report for the Committee on Aeronautical and Space Sciences, United States Senate, 1966, 36.
3. Ibid.
4. Walter A. McDougall, . . . *The Heavens and the Earth* (New York: Basic Books, 1985), 237.
5. Senate, *Soviet Space Programs, 1962–65*, 41.
6. U.S. Congress, Senate, *Soviet Space Programs, 1976–80*, Staff Report for the Committee on Commerce, Science and Transportation, United States Senate, 1985, 323.
7. Lester A. Sobel, *Space: From Sputnik to Gemini* (New York: Facts on File, 1965), 27.
8. Office of Technology Assessment (OTA), *Civilian Space Policy and Applications* (Washington, D.C.: U.S. Government Printing Office, n.d. [probably 1982]), 27.
9. As quoted in Charles Petit, "U.S. Space Agency May Never Recover," *San Francisco Chronicle*, 22 January 1987, 16.
10. John M. Logsdon, *The Decision to Go to the Moon* (Cambridge, Mass.: MIT Press, 1970), 12.
11. Ibid., 19.
12. OTA, *Civilian Space Policy and Applications*, 27–28.
13. Cass Schichtle, *The National Space Program from the Fifties into the Eighties* (Washington, D.C.: National Defense University Press, 1983), 57.
14. OTA, *Civilian Space Policy and Applications*, 4.
15. Ibid., 89.

16. Senate, *Soviet Space Programs, 1976–80*, 815.
17. Ibid., 981.
18. TASS International Service, 15 November 1985, as quoted in Nicholas L. Johnson, *The Soviet Year in Space, 1985* (Colorado Springs, Colo.: Teledyne Brown Engineering, 1986), 33.
19. Requests for information about Landsat photos can be sent to the EROS Data Center, Data Management Center, Sioux Falls, South Dakota 57198, (605) 339–2270.
20. James E. Oberg, *Red Star in Orbit* (New York: Random House, 1981), 36–37.
21. McDougall, . . . *The Heavens and the Earth*, 246.
22. Oberg, *Red Star in Orbit*, 69.
23. McDougall, . . . *The Heavens and the Earth*, 315.
24. Frank W. Anderson, Jr., *Orders of Magnitude* (Washington, D.C.: National Aeronautics and Space Administration, 1981), 28.
25. Senate, *Soviet Space Programs, 1962–65*, 106–7.
26. McDougall, . . . *The Heavens and the Earth*, 296; See also U.S. Congress, House, *United States Civilian Space Programs, 1958–1978*, Staff Report for the Subcommittee on Space Science and Applications of the Committee on Science and Technology of the U.S. House of Representatives, 1981, 384.
27. Oberg, *Red Star in Orbit*, 113.
28. U.S. Congress, Senate, *Soviet Space Programs, 1971–75*, Staff Report for the Committee on Aeronautical and Space Sciences, United States Senate, 1976, 218–19.
29. Oberg, *Red Star in Orbit*, 115.
30. *Pravda*, 2 March 1985, 2, as quoted in Johnson, *The Soviet Year in Space, 1985*, 54.
31. Petit, "U.S. Space Agency May Never Recover," 16.
32. M. Mitchell Waldrop, "NASA Council Sees Continued Erosion of Space Program," *Science*, September 5, 1986, 1035–1036.
33. Oberg, *Red Star in Orbit*, 200.
34. McDougall, . . . *The Heavens and the Earth*, 194.
35. Paul B. Stares, *The Militarization of Space* (Ithaca, N.Y.: Cornell University Press, 1985), as cited in Keith L. Nelson, "An Escalating Competition," *Science*, 1 August 1986, 581.
36. House, *United States Civilian Space Programs*, 104.

CHRONOLOGY OF LAUNCH DATES

1957	October 4	USSR: *Sputnik 1*; First artificial earth satellite
1957	November 3	USSR: *Sputnik 2*
1958	January 31	USA: *Explorer 1*; First U.S. satellite
1958	March 17	USA: *Vanguard 1*; Measured shape of earth
1958	May 14	USSR: *Sputnik 3*; Geophysical laboratory
1958	July 29	USA: National Aeronautics and Space Act
1959	January 2	USSR: *Luna 1*; First spacecraft to escape earth's gravity
1959	February 17	USA: *Vanguard 2*; First earth photo from space
1959	March 3	USA: *Pioneer 4*: Flyby of moon
1959	August 7	USA: *Explorer 6*; First TV pictures from space
1959	September 12	USSR: *Luna 2*; Impact on moon
1959	October 4	USSR: *Luna 3*; Picture of moon's far side
1960	April 1	USA: *TIROS 1*; First weather satellite
1960	April 13	USA: *Transit 1B*; First successful navigation satellite
1960	August 12	USA: *Echo 1*; First communication satellite
1961	April 12	USSR: *Vostok 1*; Gagarin, first man in space
1961	May 5	USA: *Freedom 7*; Shepard's suborbital flight

1962	February 20	USA: *Friendship 7*; Glenn's orbital flight
1962	March 7	USA: *OSO-1*; U.S.'s orbiting solar observatory
1962	March 16	USSR: *Kosmos 1*; First Soviet satellite with the Kosmos designation
1962	July 10	USA: *Telstar 1*; AT&T's first satellite
1962	August 31	USA: Communications Satellite Act (COMSAT)
1962	August 27	USA: *Mariner 2*; Flyby of Venus
1962	November 1	USSR: *Mars 1*; Flyby of Mars
1963	May 15	USA: Last Mercury flight
1963	June 16	USSR: *Vostok 6*; First woman in space
1963	July 26	USA: *Syncom 2*; First successful geosynchronous satellite
1964	June 4	USA: *Transit 5C*; Completes first operational satellite navigation system
1964	July 28	USA: *Ranger 7*; Close-up pictures of moon
1964	October 12	USSR: *Voskhod 1*; First three-man flight
1964	November 28	USA: *Mariner 4*; Mars flyby and photos
1965	March 23	USA: *Gemini 3*; First flight, Grissom and Young
1965	April 23	USSR: *Molniya 1*; Probably first Soviet communication satellite
1965	November 16	USSR: *Venera 3*; Impact on Venus
1966	January 31	USSR: *Luna 9*; Soft landing, photos from moon
1966	March 31	USSR: *Luna 10*; Orbits the moon
1966	May 30	USA: *Surveyor 1*; Soft landing on the moon
1966	June 25	USSR: *Kosmos 122*; Probably first Soviet weather satellite
1966	August 10	USA: *Orbiter 1*; Pictures of moon from orbit
1966	November 11	USA: *Gemini 12*; Last Gemini flight
1966	December 6	USA: *ATS-1*; First Applications Technology Satellite
1967	January 27	USA: *Apollo 204*; Death of three astronauts in cabin fire
1967	April 17	USA: *Surveyor 3*; Samples from lunar surface
1967	April 23	USSR: *Soyuz 1* flight; Komarov killed
1968	October 11	USA: *Apollo 7*; First manned Apollo flight
1968	December 7	USA: *OAO-2*; Orbiting Astrophysical Observatory
1968	December 21	USA: *Apollo 8*; First circumlunar flight
1969	March 27	USSR: *Meteor 1*; First Soviet weather satellite in this series

1969	July 16	USA: *Apollo 11*; First landing on the moon
1969	October 14	USSR: *Interkosmos 1*; First flight in the Interkosmos series
1970	April 11	USA: *Apollo 13*; Near-disaster flight
1970	August 17	USSR: *Venera 7*; Soft landing on Venus
1970	September 12	USSR: *Luna 16*; Lunar soil samples returned to earth
1970	November 10	USSR: *Luna 17*; Unmanned lunar rover
1971	April 19	USSR: *Salyut 1*; First space station
1971	May 19	USSR: *Mars 2*; Impact on surface of Mars
1971	May 28	USSR: *Mars 3*; Mars orbit
1971	May 30	USA: *Mariner 9*; Mars orbit with photos
1971	July 26	USA: *Apollo 15*; First manned lunar rover
1971	November 15	USSR: Signing of Intersputnik agreement
1972	March 3	USA: *Pioneer 10*; Jupiter flyby
1972	April 14	USSR: *Prognoz 1*; First in series of satellites to conduct solar research
1972	July 23	USA: *ERTS 1*; First earth resources satellite
1972	August 21	USA: *OAO-C*; Orbiting astronomical telescope
1973	April 6	USA: *Pioneer 11*; Saturn flyby
1973	May 25	USA: *Skylab 2*; First manned skylab
1973	November 3	USA: *Mariner 10*; First photos of Mercury
1975	June 8	USSR: *Venera 9*; Photos from surface of Venus
1975	July 15	USA/USSR: Apollo-Soyuz Test Project
1975	August 20 and September 9	USA: *Viking 1* and *2*; Experiments on Martian surface
1976	February 19	USA: *Marisat 1*; First commercial maritime communication satellite
1977	August 20	USA: *Voyager 2*; Flyby of Jupiter, Saturn, Uranus, and Neptune
1977	September 29	USSR: *Salyut 6*; Second-generation space station
1978	February 22	USA: *Navstar 1*; First flight of new navigation system
1978	June 27	USA: *SeaSat 1*; First ocean resources satellite
1979	March	USA: First photos of Jupiter and its moons by *Voyagers 1* and 2
1979	July 11	USA: Reentry and destruction of Skylab

1979	December 24	ESA: First successful satellite launch by the European Space Agency
1980	November	USA: First photos of Saturn and its moons by *Voyager 1*
1981	April 12	USA: First manned flight of a reusable spacecraft (*STS-1*)
1981	August	USA: First photos of Saturn and its moons by *Voyager 2*
1981	October 20 and November 4	USSR: Launch of *Venera 13* and *14* to Venus; soft-landing on Venus on March 1 and 5, 1982
1982	April 19	USSR: *Salyut 7*
1982	November 11	USA: *STS-5*; First operational flight of space shuttle
1983	June 2 and 7	USSR: *Venera 15* and *16*; Venus orbit
1983	June 18	USA: *STS-7*; First U.S. woman in space, Sally Ride
1983	June 27	USSR: *Soyuz T-9*; First construction in space
1983	November 28	USA: *STS-9*; First Spacelab mission
1984	February 8	USSR: *Soyuz T-10/11*; 237-day flight in extravehicular activity
1984	July 17	USSR: *Soyuz T-12*; First woman EVA
1984	December 15 and 21	USSR: *VEGA 1* and 2; Flyby of Halley's comet
1985	June 6	USSR: *Soyuz T-13*; Repair of *Salyut 7*
1986	January 28	USA: Shuttle *Challenger* explosion
1986	February 20	USSR: *Mir* space station

SELECTED BIBLIOGRAPHY

Four magazines are invaluable sources of information on space. These are *Space World*, *Spaceflight*, *Space Education*, and *Aviation Week & Space Technology*. In addition, the National Aeronautics and Space Administration (NASA) has published more than one hundred books, pamphlets and reports covering every aspect of the United States space program. Regional NASA offices and U.S. Government Printing Office bookstores carry a complete list of these items and have the most popular titles in stock. Libraries often carry a number of the NASA publications also.

Allen, Joseph P. *Entering Space: An Astronaut's Odyssey*. New York: Stewart, Tabori, and Chang, 1984.

Anderson, Frank W., Jr. *Orders of Magnitude*. Washington, D.C.: NASA, 1981.

Brooks, Courtney G., James M. Grimwood, and Loyd S. Swenson, Jr. *Chariots for Apollo*. Washington, D.C.: NASA, 1979.

Clarke, Arthur C. *Man and Space*. New York: Time, 1964.

Compton, W. David, and Charles D. Benson. *Living and Working in Space*. Washington, D.C.: NASA, 1983.

Crooke, Wilson W., Ill. "Gagarin, The First." *Space World*, April 1986, pp. 25–27.

————. "Zond: The Soviet Manned Moon Program." *Space World*, March 1986, pp. 28–31.

Daniloff, Nicholas. *The Kremlin and the Cosmos*. New York: Knopf, 1972.

Diamond, Edwin. *The Rise and Fall of the Space Age*. Garden City, N.Y.: Doubleday, 1964.

Dorr, Les, Jr. "The Salvage of Salyut 7." *Space World*, May 1986, pp. 8–12.

———. "Orbital Weather Watchers: 25 Years after TIROS." *Space World*, May 1985, pp. 7–9.

Garelik, Glenn. " 'Our Boys Are Dead.' " *Discover*, April 1986, pp. 59–65.

Hanle, Paul A. "The Beeping Ball that Started a Dash into Outer Space." *Smithsonian*, October 1982, pp. 148–167.

Herres, Robert T. "The Military Use of Space." *Vital Speeches of the Day*, November 15, 1986, pp. 74–77.

Johnson, Nicholas L. *The Soviet Year in Space, 1986*. Colorado Springs, Colo.: Teledyne Brown Engineering, 1987.

Lewis, Richard S. "Explorer I: The Second Age of Discovery." *Space Education*, October 1983, pp. 256–259.

Longsdon, John M. *The Decision to Go to the Moon*. Cambridge, Mass.: The MIT Press, 1970.

Mammana, Dennis L. "Space Telescope: The Beginning of an Era." *Space World*, August 1985, pp. 21–23 +.

McDougall, Walter A. . . . *The Heavens and the Earth*. New York: Basic Books, 1985.

"NASA's First 25 Years." *Space World*, October 1983, pp. 25–32.

Nicks, Oran W. *Far Travelers*. Washington, D.C.: NASA, 1985.

Oberg, James E. *Red Star in Orbit*. New York: Random House, 1981.

Oberg, James E. *The New Race for Space*. Harrisburg, Pa.: Stackpole Books, 1984.

Office of Technology Assessment (OTA). *Civilian Space Policy and Applications*. Washington, D.C.: U.S. Government Printing Office, n.d. (probably, 1982).

———. *Salyut: Soviet Steps toward Permanent Human Presence in Space*. Washington, D.C.: Government Printing Office, 1983.

———. *Civilian Space Stations and the U.S. Future in Space*. Washington, D.C.: NASA, 1984.

Osman, Tony. *Space History*. New York: St. Martin's Press, 1983.

Riabchikov, Evgeny. *Russians in Space*. Garden City, N.Y.: Doubleday, 1971.

Schichtle, Cass. *The National Space Program from the Fifties into the Eighties*. Washington, D.C.: National Defense University Press, 1983.

Shelton, William. *Soviet Space Exploration: The First Decade*. New York: Washington Square Press, 1968.

Simpson, Clive. "NASA's First 25 Years." *Space Education*, October 1984, pp. 346–349.

Smith, W. L., et al. "The Meteorological Satellite: An Overview of 25 Years of Operations." *Science*, January 31, 1986, pp. 455–462.

Sobel, Lester A. *Space: From Sputnik to Gemini*. New York: Facts on File, 1965.

"Special Report: Europe's Maturing Space Programs." *Aviation Week & Space Technology*, June 9, 1986.

Stares, Paul B. *The Militarization of Space*. Ithaca, N.Y.: Cornell University Press, 1985.

"The 'Space Age': 25 Years and Counting." *Sky and Telescope*, October 1982.

U.S. Congress, House. *United States Civilian Space Programs, 1958–1978*, Staff Report for the Subcommittee on Space Science and Applications of the Committee on Science and Technology of the U.S. House of Representatives, 1981 (2 parts).

U.S. Congress, Senate. *Soviet Space Programs, 1976–80*, Staff Report for the Committee on Commerce, Science and Transportation, United States Senate, 1985 (3 parts). Similar reports were published for the periods 1962–65, 1966–70, and 1971–1975.

Waldrop, M. Mitchell. "A Soviet Plan for Exploring the Planets." *Science*, May 10, 1985, pp. 698–699.

INDEX

IN MEMORY OF

YURI GAGARIN

FIRST MAN IN SPACE, APRIL 12, 1961

FROM THE ASTRONAUTS OF THE
UNITED STATES OF AMERICA.

JOHN H. GLENN, Jr.
for
MERCURY ASTRONAUTS

JAMES A. McDIVITT
for
GEMINI ASTRONAUTS

NEIL ARMSTRONG
for
APOLLO ASTRONAUTS

ABOUT
THE AUTHOR

David E. Newton has taught science and mathematics at nearly every grade level, from elementary through post-graduate. He is formerly professor of chemistry at Salem (Mass.) State College and visiting professor of science education at Western Washington University. He is currently adjunct professor in the College of Professional Studies at the University of San Francisco, where he teaches a course in Science and Social Issues.

Dr. Newton is the author of thirty-five books and over three hundred other publications.

387.8
New

Newton, David E.
U.S. and Soviet
space programs

$12.90

DATE			

STEPHENSON HIGH SCHOOL
133 BARTELL ST
STEPHENSON, MI
498870000

03/09/90   12.90

              685974   05042